FINANCIAL ANALYSIS:
A Programmed Approach

FINANCIAL ANALYSIS:
A Programmed Approach

Neil Seitz

St. Louis University

RESTON PUBLISHING COMPANY, INC.
A Prentice-Hall Company
Reston, Virginia

Library of Congress Cataloging in Publication Data

Seitz, Neil E.
    Financial analysis.

    1. Business enterprises–Finance–Programmed
instruction. I. Title.
HF5550.S3724 658.1'513'077   75-34364
ISBN 0-87909-286-6

© 1976 by Reston Publishing Company, Inc.
A Prentice-Hall Company
Reston, Virginia 22090

10 9 8 7 6 5 4 3 2 1

PRINTED IN THE UNITED STATES OF AMERICA

CONTENTS

INTRODUCTION

Financial analysis provides the basis for much of financial decision making. The book is directed primarily to the needs of the manager of a nonfinancial company; that is, a company involved in the production and/or delivery of goods and services, such as a clothing store or an automobile manufacturer, as opposed to a company involved in the provision of financial services, such as a bank. Many of the techniques are, however, applicable to other types of financial work, such as security analysis or commercial loan analysis.

The kinds of financial decisions faced by widely diverse types of nonfinancial companies are actually quite similar. These decisions fall into two broad categories. On the one hand, the financial manager is responsible for raising the necessary funds to operate the business. On the other hand, he is increasingly involved with the decision as to where these funds should be invested in the firm. These are the two primary areas of financial decision making and the manager must act in such a way as to further the goals of the firm.

This material is presented primarily from the viewpoint of the financial manager. In a large corporation, the financial manager will most likely carry the title of vice president-finance. For a small company, one person may have the duties of president and chief operating officer as well as financial manager. People at other levels and locations in the firm are also involved in financial decisions. All managers are concerned with profitability. All divisions of the firm are involved in capital budgeting proposals and capital budgeting decisions. All divisions are also involved in the analysis of their past operating results and the projection of their future operating results. Therefore, the techniques of financial analysis are valuable not only to the financial manager and his staff, but to those at all levels of the business organization.

What are the goals toward which financial management strives? The financial manager, as well as the other managers of the firm, operate primarily on behalf of its owners. For the corporation, the owners are the equity holders. The portion of the owners' welfare under the influence of the financial manager is their wealth. The financial manager therefore acts to maximize the wealth of the owners by maximizing the value of their investment in the company. Maximization of value is then the goal of financial management.

There are certain specific guidelines the financial manager follows in pursuing this goal. First, he attempts to raise funds for the firm at the lowest cost possible, given the riskiness of the firm's asset structure. Second, he attempts to guide the use of these funds within the firm to the highest returns possible, consistent with risk considerations. Risk is critical to the determination of returns required by investors and therefore has a major effect on value. Investors generally dislike risk and expect higher returns as compensation for accepting risk. Therefore, in pursuing the goal of value maximization, the manager must attempt to make the optimal trade-off between risk and return.

This textbook is aimed at the development of the necessary financial analysis for practical business decisions. It is not a book on finance theory: proofs are not given, and esoteric topics with little practical application are avoided. The book is also lacking in materials describing the financial institutions and instruments in use today. Instead, it concentrates on the techniques that will aid in analyzing financial data and making financial decisions.

The first chapters of this text cover the methods of analyzing past financial results and forecasting the results of future operations. These are basic tools required for decision making. Leverage, or the relationship between fixed and variable costs, is covered next. Leverage affects both the profitability and risk of the firm. Following this, the techniques of analysis for decisions relative to working capital management, or the management of current assets and current liabilities, are covered. The chapters on time value of money and capital budgeting are the basis for decisions relative to the fixed assets of the firm. The final two chapters cover the determination of value and the estimation of the cost of funds to the firm.

A final guideline for the user of this text: financial analysis is not a goal in itself; financial analysis is a means to an end; that end is financial decision making. A clear understanding of the decision being faced and how the analysis about to be performed will weigh on that decision can eliminate many of the potential difficulties encountered in financial analysis.

NEIL SEITZ

HOW TO USE THIS BOOK

Place a card over the answers at the bottom of each page before beginning. You will be asked to respond at numerous points. After each response, uncover the correct answer and check it against your response. Do this after each response. Do not wait until the end of a frame to check your answers. If your response was not correct, try to understand the correct answer before continuing. The most frequently missed questions are followed by an explanation of the correct answer and additional exercises on the same topic.

1

FINANCIAL STATEMENT ANALYSIS

The logical place to begin the mastery of financial analysis is with the analysis of financial statements. The basic data with which the analyst must work is found in the financial statements. So the ability to understand, interpret, and use this information is basic to an understanding of finance.

The financial statements used here are the income statement and balance sheet. If you have not had a course in accounting or do not have a basic understanding of financial statements, a review of this material is recommended.

The purposes of financial statement analysis are many and varied. The analyst may be a potential trade creditor or a bank officer considering a short-term loan, or he may be a long-term creditor such as a bondholder. The analyst could also be a manager or owner of the company. Each of the users of financial statements will be interested in different types of information. The short-term creditor will be interested in the ability of the company to repay the debt within a short period of time. The long-term creditor, on the other hand, will be interested in the ability of the company to generate the necessary profits for repayment over a number of years. The creditor will also be interested in his protection in the case of default. The owner is interested in both the profitability and safety of his investment. The manager is interested in the profitability of the company, the efficiency with which assets are used, and the risk to which the company is exposed. Each will use the financial statements to discern the condition and trend of the company relative to his area of interest.

Just as there are many different users of financial statements, there are various methods of analysis. In this treatment, the method of ratio analysis will be used. Suppose that profits for ABC Company are 50% greater than those for XYZ Company. Should ABC be proud of this accomplishment? To answer this question, you must also know some other things. Suppose, for example, ABC has twice the sales and three times the total assets of XYZ. The shareholders of ABC may not be happy with this performance. They would not be interested in profit alone but in profit relative to other things, such as assets committed or shares of common stock outstanding. In other words, they would be interested in the *ratio* of profit to something else. Likewise, the ratio of debt to total assets frequently means more than the simple dollar amount of debt. The shareholders would want to compare the ratio to that of another similar company or to that of the same company for a previous year.

There are various categories of ratios. *Liquidity* ratios are used to measure the ability to meet maturing obligations in the near future. *Activity* ratios are used to evaluate the level of asset commitment and the efficiency of asset usage. *Leverage* ratios help in evaluating the use of debt financing and, finally, *profitability* ratios are used to evaluate the degree to which the other activities result in profits. By using these ratios singly or in combination, the analyst is able to develop an understanding of the strengths and weaknesses of the company that are of particular interest to him.

In this chapter, you learn how to compute and interpret twelve widely used ratios and how to use them in combination to evaluate a company and spot potential problems. Upon completing this chapter, you will understand the basics of financial statement analysis.

A. INTRODUCTION TO RATIOS

1. Ratios are used to make information comparable between financial statements. A ratio can be compared to figures for another company, an industry average, or the figures for the same company for previous years.

2. As pointed out in the introduction to this chapter, there are four main categories of ratios;

   _____ ratios are used to measure the ability to meet maturing obligations in the near future.

   _____ratios are used to evaluate the use of debt financing.

   _____ratios are used to evaluate the level of asset commitment and the efficiency of asset usage.

_____ratios are used to evaluate the degree to which the activities of the company result in profits.

3. In the following sections each category of ratios will be discussed in sequence. Following that, the ratios will be brought together as a system to be used in evaluating a company. The 1973 through 1975 financial statements for Office Supply Corporation appear on pages 3 and 4. You will need to refer to these frequently throughout the chapter.

B. LIQUIDITY RATIOS

4. _____ratios are used to measure the ability of the company to meet maturing obligations in the near future. The two main liquidity ratios are the current ratio and the acid test ratio.

5. The current ratio is defined as current assets divided by current liabilities. The current ratio is used as an indicator of the ability of the company to meet cash obligations in the near future. It indicates the extent to which current liabilities are covered by assets that are most rapidly liquidated, or converted to cash. The 1974 current ratio for Office Supply was:

Current Ratio =   Current Assets   =   50   =
                   Current Liabilities   30   _____

OFFICE SUPPLY CORPORATION
INCOME STATEMENTS / YEARS ENDING DECEMBER 31

	1973	1974	1975
Sales	$ 80	$100	$120
Cost of Goods Sold	40	50	60
Gross Profit	40	50	60
Administrative and Overhead Expense	25	30	36
Net Operating Income	15	20	24
Interest	1	2	6
Earnings Before Tax	14	18	18
Tax	7	9	9
Net Income	$ 7	$ 9	$ 9

2. Liquidity   4. Liquidity
   Leverage
   Activity   5. 1.67
   Profitability

OFFICE SUPPLY CORPORATION / Balance sheets / December 31

ASSETS	1973	1974	1975
Cash	$ 8	$ 10	$ 10
Accounts Receivable	16	20	50
Inventory	16	20	30
Total Current Assets	40	50	90
Fixed Assets (net of depreciation)	40	50	60
Total Assets	$ 80	$100	$150

LIABILITIES AND NET WORTH			
Accounts Payable	$ 10	$ 15	$ 20
Miscellaneous Accruals	10	15	20
Total Current Liabilities	20	30	40
Long Term Debt	10	20	60
Common Stock	10	10	10
Paid-in Capital	10	10	10
Retained Earnings	30	30	30
Total Liabilities and Net Worth	$ 80	$100	$150

6. The 1975 current ratio for Office Supply was _____ .

Skip to Frame 8 if you got the correct answer.

7. Current assets for 1975 were $_____ and current liabilities were
   $_____ . Using the formula in Frame 5, the current ratio for 1975
   was 90/40 = _____. The 1973 current ratio was _____.

8. Generally, the higher the current ratio the more liquid the company.
   Office Supply's 1975 current ratio was *higher/lower* than its 1974 current
   ratio. Therefore, it appears to be *more/less* liquid at the end of 1975,
   compared to 1974.

---

6. 90/40 = 2.25

7. 90
   40
   2.25
   40/20 = 2

8. higher
   more

9. The current ratio recognizes all current assets. The primary current assets are Cash, Marketable Securities, Accounts Receivable, and Inventory. Of these items, inventory would be the most difficult to convert to cash quickly during a business downturn. For this reason, the *acid test* ratio (also called the *quick* ratio) is frequently used in conjunction with the current ratio. The acid test ratio considers current assets other than inventory. For 1974 Office Supply's acid test ratio was:

$$\text{Acid Test Ratio} = \frac{\text{Current Assets} - \text{Inventory}}{\text{Current Liabilities}} = \frac{50 - 20}{30} =$$

_____

_____

10. The 1975 Acid Test Ratio was _____ .

Skip to Frame 12 if you got the correct answer.

11. Refer again to the formula for the acid test ratio in Frame 9. Current assets for 1975 were $_____ and inventory was $_____ . Current liabilities were $_____ . Therefore, the acid test ratio was $(90 - 30) \div 40 =$ _____ . For 1973, the acid test ratio was _____ .

12. A higher acid test ratio indicates that the company is more liquid, or is in a better position to meet its current obligations. The acid test ratio would indicate that Office Supply was *more/less* liquid in 1975 than in 1974.

13. The current ratio and the acid test ratio are used in combination as indicators of _____ or ability to meet maturing obligations in the near future. Higher current ratios and acid test ratios indicate *greater/less* liquidity.

---

9. $30/30 = 1$

10. $(90\text{-}30)/40 = 1.5$

11. $90
    30
    40
    1.5
    $(40\text{-}60)/20 = 1.2$

12. more

13. liquidity
    greater

C. LEVERAGE RATIOS

14. The sources of funds available to a company are divided between debt and equity. Debt, of course, is a fixed cost sources of funds. If the return on funds employed in the business is greater than the cost, the difference accrues to the equity holders. Risk, however, is increased because the company must meet debt obligations even if business conditions are bad. The leverage ratios indicate the extent of debt usage and the ability of the company to meet debt obligations. The leverage ratios to be used here are the *debt* ratio (also called debt to total assets ratio) and *times interest earned*.

15. The debt ratio is defined as total debt divided by total assets. It indicates the percent of assets that are financed through debt. For 1974, Office Supply's debt ratio was:

$$\text{Debt Ratio} = \frac{\text{Total Debt}}{\text{Total Assets}} = \frac{50 *}{100} = \underline{\hspace{3cm}}$$

$$\underline{\hspace{3cm}}$$

* Current liabilities are part of total debt.

16. The 1975 debt ratio was _____ .

Skip to Frame 18 if you got the correct answer.

17. Refer again to the formula for the debt ratio in Frame 15. Once again, total debt includes long term debt and current liabilities. Total debt for Office Supply in 1975 was $40 + $60 = _____ and total assets were _____ . The debt ratio, therefore, was 100/150 = _____ . The debt ratio for 1973 was _____ .

---

15. 0.5

16. $(40 + 60) / 150 = .67$

17. $100
    150
    .67
    $(20 + 10) / 80 =$
    .375

18. The debt ratio indicates what percent of the assets are financed through debt. In 1974, 50% of the assets were financed with debt compared to _____% in 1975. Office Supply, therefore, used *more/less* financial leverage in 1975 than in 1974.

19. The ability of the company to meet interest payments is of particular concern. The *times interest earned* ratio is used as an indication of the ability to meet interest payments. It is defined as (Earnings before tax + Interest) ÷ Interest. In 1974, the times interest earned for Office Supply was:

$$\text{Times Interest Earned} = \frac{\text{Earnings before tax + Interest}}{\text{Interest}} = \frac{18 + 2}{2} =$$

_____

_____

20. The times interest earned ratio for 1975 was _____ .

Skip to Frame 22 if you got the correct answer.

21. Earnings before tax for 1975 were $_____ and interest was _____ so profit before tax and interest was $18 + 6 = $_____ .Times interest earned, therefore, was 24/6 = _____ . Times interest earned for 1973 was _____ .

22. The greater the times interest earned, the greater the decline in profit the company could take and still meet its interest payments. Times interest earned *increased/decreased* from 1974 to 1975. Therefore, Office Supply has become *more/less* vulnerable in the case of a profit decline.

---

18. 67%
    more
19. 10
20. (18 + 6) /6 = 4
21. $18
    6
    24
    4
    (14 + 1) /1 = 15
22. decreased
    more

D. ACTIVITY RATIOS

23. _____ ratios are used to measure the level of asset commitment and the degree of asset usage. Activity ratios give an indication of the *efficiency* of asset usage. The activity ratios to be discussed here are *inventory turnover, average collection period, fixed asset turnover*, and *total asset turnover*.

24. The inventory turnover ratio is defined as sales divided by inventory. It is used as a measure of the efficiency of inventory usage. It indicates how many dollars of sales the company was able to generate for each dollar of inventory. The 1974 inventory turnover for Office Supply was $100/20 =$ _____ .

25. Office Supply's inventory turnover for 1975 was _____ .

Skip to Frame 27 if you got the correct answer.

26. Note again that inventory turnover is defined as sales ÷ inventory. For 1975, sales were $_____ and inventory was $_____ . Inventory turnover, therefore, was $120/30 =$ _____ . In 1973 Office Supply's inventory turnover was _____ .

27. Higher inventory turnover is generally thought of as indicating more efficient use of inventory in generating sales (although extremely high inventory turnover might result in lost sales due to lack of merchandise availability). Inventory turnover *increased/decreased* from 1974 to 1975. It would appear that Office Supply was *more/less* efficient in inventory usage in 1975 compared to 1974.

---

23. Activity

24. 5

25. $120/30 = 4$

26. $120
      30
      4
      80/16 = 5$

27. decreased
      less

28. The average collection period indicates the average number of days between the sale of a product and the receipt of payment. The average collection period is computed as 365 x (accounts receivable / sales). For Office Supply, the average collection period in 1974 was:

Average Collection Period = 365 x $\frac{20}{100}$ = _____ days.

29. For 1975, the average collection period was _____ .

Skip to Frame 31 if you got the correct answer.

30. Refer to the formula in Frame 28. Using that formula, the average collection period for 1975 was:

Average Collection Period = 365 x $\frac{50}{120}$ = 152 days.

The average collection period for 1973 was _____ .

31. An increase in the average collection period indicates that customers are becoming slower in paying their bills. The average collection period *increased/decreased* from 1974 to 1975. If the average collection period is greater than that allowed under the company's credit terms, it indicates that customers are not paying their bills when due. If Office Supply is selling on 60-day credit terms, we know that many customers were overdue in 1974 and *more / less* were overdue in 1975.

32. The fixed asset turnover ratio is an indicator of the amount of sales that are generated per dollar of fixed assets. It does not indicate that fixed assets were physically "turned over." Fixed assets turnover is defined as sales ÷ fixed assets. In 1974 the fixed asset turnover for Office Supply was:

Fixed Asset Turnover = $\frac{Sales}{Fixed\ Assets}$ = $\frac{100}{50}$ = _____ .

---

28. 73

29. 365 x (50/120) = *152* days

30. 365 x (16/80) = *73* days

31. increased
    more

32. 2

33. Fixed asset turnover for 1975 was _____ .

    Skip to Frame 35 if you got the correct answer.

34. Fixed asset turnover for 1973 was _____ .

35. An increase in fixed asset turnover indicates that the company was able to generate *more / less* sales per dollar of fixed assets. In 1975, Office Supply generated *more / the same / less* sales per dollar of fixed assets as in 1974. This would tend to indicate that they used fixed assets with the same efficiency in both years.

36. Total asset turnover is a summary of the uses of individual classes of assets. It is used as an overall indicator of the efficiency of asset usage. Total asset turnover for Office Supply in 1974 was:

    $$\text{Total Asset Turnover} = \frac{\text{Sales}}{\text{Total Assets}} = \frac{100}{100} = \underline{\hspace{1.5cm}} .$$

37. Total asset turnover for 1975 was _____ .

    Skip to Frame 39 if you got the correct answer.

38. Total asset turnover for 1973 was _____ .

39. A decrease in total asset turnover is the result of a decrease in sales per dollar of assets. This would generally indicate decreased efficiency of asset usage. Total asset turnover for Office Supply *increased / decreased* from 1974 to 1975. This would indicate that Office Supply became *more / less* efficient in asset usage.

---

33. $120/60 = 2$

34. $80/40 = 2$

35. more
    the same

36. 1

37. $120/150 = .80$

38. $80/80 = 1$

39. decreased
    less

E. PROFITABILITY RATIOS

40. _____ ratios are used to measure the ability of the company to turn sales into profits and to earn profits on assets committed. The primary profitability ratios are the *operating profit margin, earning power,* and *return on net worth.*

41. The operating profit margin looks at profit from operations *before* any return to the sources of funds. It is not affected by the method of financing. Operating profit margin is defined as net operating income ÷ sales. For 1974, Office Supply's operating profit margin was:

$$\text{Operating Profit Margin} = \frac{\text{Net Operating Income}}{\text{Sales}} = \frac{20}{100} = \underline{\hspace{1.5cm}}.$$

42. For 1975, the operating profit margin was _____ .

Skip to Frame 44 if you got the correct answer.

43. For 1975, net operating income was $_____ and sales were $_____ . The operating profit margin was 24/120 = _____%. For 1973, the operating profit margin was _____%.

44. The operating profit margin for 1975 was *less than / the same as / greater than* for 1974. In 1975, the company was as efficient as in 1974 in converting sales to operating income. There is, therefore, no evidence of a decline in operating efficiency.

45. The net profit margin is an indicator of the company's ability to convert sales to profit after tax. Unlike the operating profit margin, the net profit margin considers profit after tax and interest payments. The net profit

---

40. Profitability

41. 20%

42. 24/120 = *20%*

43. $24
$120
20%
15/80 = *18.75%*

44. the same as

margin is defined as profit after tax ÷ sales. For 1974, Office Supply's net profit margin was:

$$\text{Net Profit Margin} = \frac{\text{Profit After Tax}}{\text{Sales}} = \frac{9}{100} = \underline{\hspace{2cm}}.$$

46. For 1975, the net profit margin was _____%.

Skip to Frame 48 if you got the correct answer.

47. For 1975, profit after tax was $_____ and sales were $_____.
The net profit margin, therefore, was 9/120 = _____%. The net profit margin for 1973 was _____%.

48. The net profit margin declined from _____% in 1974 to _____% in 1975. This indicates an *increase / decrease* in their ability to convert sales to profit after tax. You might further note that the operating profit margin was 20% each year and the tax rate was 50% each year. The decline in net profit margin was apparently caused by increased interest expense.

49. The *earning power* measures the proportion of net operating income to assets committed. It is another indicator of efficiency of asset usage. Earning power is defined as net operating income ÷ total assets. Office Supply's 1974 earning power was:

$$\text{Earning Power} = \frac{\text{Net Operating Income}}{\text{Total Assets}} = \frac{20}{100} = \underline{\hspace{2cm}}\%.$$

50. The 1975 earning power was _____%.

Skip to Frame 52 if you got the correct answer.

---

45. 9%

46. 9/120 = *7.5%*

47. $9
$120
7.5%
7/80 = *8.75%*

48. 9%
7.5%
decrease

49. 20%

50. 24/150 = *16%*

51. Net operating income for 1975 was \$_____ and total assets were \$_____. Earning power, defined as net operating income ÷ total assets, was 24/150 = _____%. For 1973, earning power was _____%.

52. From 1974 to 1975, earning power *increased / declined.* The company was able to generate *more / less* net operating income per dollar of assets. This indicates that the company did not use its assets as profitably in 1975 as in 1974.

53. The owners are particularly interested in the return on their investment. This is measured with the *return on net worth* ratio. Return on net worth is defined as Net Income ÷ Net Worth. Net worth represents the book value of the owners' investment. For Office Supply, net worth equals common stock plus paid-in capital plus retained earnings. For 1974, net worth was \$10 + \$10 + \$30 = \$_____ and return on net worth was:

$$\text{Return on Net Worth} = \frac{\text{Net Income}}{\text{Net Worth}} = \frac{9}{50} = \underline{\hspace{2cm}}\%.$$

54. For 1975, return on net worth was _____%.

Skip to Frame 56 if you got the correct answer.

55. For 1975, net worth was \$10 + \$10 + \$30 = \$_____ and net income was \$_____. Return on net worth, therefore, was _____%. For 1973, return on net worth was _____%.

---

51. \$24
   \$150
   16%
   15/80 = *18.75%*

52. declined
   less

53. \$50
   9/50 = *18%*

54. 9/50 = *18%*

55. \$50
   \$9
   9/50 = *18%*
   7/50 = *14%*

56. Return on net worth *increased / remained constant / decreased* from 1974 to 1975. The shareholders would probably be somewhat disappointed that the 20% increase in sales did not result in increased return on their investment.

F. THE PROFITABILITY SYSTEM

57. The purpose of this section is to show how ratios can be used in combination to analyze a company. While various systems of ratios can be used depending on the analyst's point of view, the approach here will be to analyze Office Supply from the point of view of the shareholders. You noted in Frame 56 that return on net worth for 1975 did not increase with the increase in sales. This would be received as disappointing news by the shareholders.

58. There are two possible explanations of this failure to increase return on net worth. For increased sales to result in increased return on net worth with no change in the tax rate, it is necessary for one of two things to happen. Either the increased sales must result in increased earning power or the company must have used financial leverage to better advantage. It is necessary to see what did happen in the areas of debt usage and earning power.

59. The first area to check is the use of debt, or financial leverage. As this topic will be discussed in more detail in Chapter 3, it is sufficient here to point out that the average interest rate on debt in both 1974 and 1975 was 10% (2/20 = 10% and 6/60 = 10%) and that the debt ratio went from _____% in 1974 to _____% in 1975. Since the company used more financial leverage in 1975 than in 1974 and paid the same interest rate on debt, it would not appear that the unfavorable use of financial leverage was the cause of their failure to increase return on net worth. If earning power remained constant, an increase in the debt ratio without an increase in the *rate* of interest would normally be expected to increase return on net worth. It is necessary to look beyond the debt ratio for Office Supply's difficulties.

---

56. remained constant

59. 50%
     66.6%

60. The one remaining possibility is the earning power. You will recall that earning power declined from ⎯⎯⎯⎯⎯% in 1974 to ⎯⎯⎯⎯⎯% in 1975. It would appear, then, that the failure to improve return on net worth was caused by a decline in ⎯⎯⎯⎯⎯⎯⎯⎯ ⎯⎯⎯⎯⎯⎯⎯⎯ . If the decline in earning power had not been offset by an increase in the debt ratio, the company would have suffered a decline in return on net worth.

61. This portion of the search for the cause of Office Supply's failure to increase return on net worth can be summarized in a simple chart.

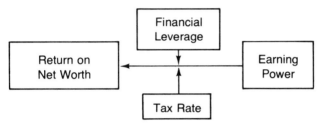

Earning Power represents the result of operations. Through the use of financial leverage, and through payment of taxes, earning power is translated through to return on net worth.

62. Since a decline in earning power was the factor keeping return on net worth from increasing, the next step would be to determine what factors caused this decline. Recall that earning power is defined as net operating income ÷ total assets. Earning power can also be defined as follows:

$$\text{Earning Power} = \frac{\text{Net Operating Income}}{\text{Total Assets}}$$

$$= \frac{\text{Net Operating Income}}{\text{Sales}} \quad X \quad \frac{\text{Sales}}{\text{Total Assets}}$$

$$= \text{Operating Profit Margin X Total Asset Turnover.}$$

A review of the definitions of operating profit margin and total asset turnover in Frames 36 and 41 will verify this approach. We can therefore say that:

Earning Power = Operating Profit Margin X ⎯⎯⎯⎯⎯⎯⎯⎯⎯⎯⎯⎯⎯⎯⎯

---

60. 20%
16%
earning power

62. Total Asset Turnover

63. The decline in earning power, therefore, must have been caused by either a decline in _____ _____ _____ or a decline in _____ _____ _____ . The next step is to find which of these occurred.

64. The operating profit margin was _____% in 1974 and _____% in 1975. The decline in earning power *was / was not* caused by a decline in the operating profit margin.

65. Total asset turnover was _____ in 1974 and _____ in 1975. Therefore, it appears that the decline in earning power *was / was not* caused by a decline in total asset turnover.

66. At this point, the chart in Frame 61 can be extended to show the additional analysis.

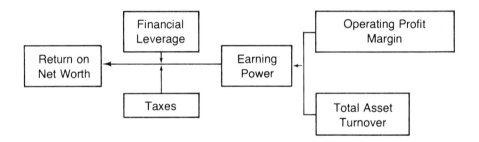

Return on net worth depends on earning power, taxes, and _____ _____ . Earning power, in turn, depends on operating profit margin and _____ _____ _____ .

---

63. Operating Profit Margin
    Total Asset Turnover

64. 20%
    20%
    was not

65. 1
    .8
    was

66. Financial Leverage
    Total Asset Turnover

67. Total asset turnover, of course, can be broken down according to the individual asset classifications. Use the table below to summarize asset turnover.

Ratio	1974	1975
Total Asset Turnover	1	.8
Fixed Asset Turnover		
Inventory Turnover		
Average Collection Period		

68. From 1974 to 1975, fixed asset turnover *increased / remain unchanged / decreased*. Therefore, the decline in total asset turnover and earning power *was /was not* caused by a change in fixed asset turnover.

69. Inventory turnover, on the other hand, *increased / decreased* so inventory turnover was at least part of the problem.

70. The average collection period *increased / decreased* from 1974 to 1975 so increased investment in accounts receivable was also part of the problem.

71. The disappointing performance of Office Supply was caused by a decline in _____ turnover and an increase in _____ _____ _____ . Due to the additional funds tied up in inventory and accounts receivable, total asset turnover declined and in turn earning power declined. Increased financial leverage balanced against the decrease in earning power to give a return on net worth that did not change from 1974 to 1975.

67.

	1974	1975	For Review:
Fixed Asset Turnover	2	2	Frame 32
Inventory Turnover	5	4	Frame 24
Average Collection Period	73	152	Frame 28

68. remained unchanged
was not

69. decreased

70. increased

71. inventory
average collection period

72. The preceding is one example of how ratios can be used as a system to analyze a company. The ratio system used in analyzing profitability is completed in the following chart:

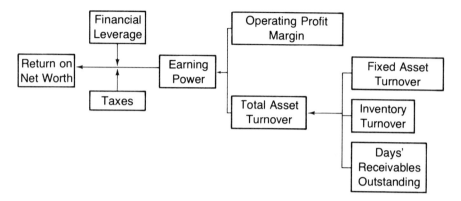

Total asset turnover represents the combined effects of asset turnover for the individual asset classifications and earning power represented by the combined effects of total asset turnover and operating profit margin. Through financial leverage and taxes, earning power is translated to return on net worth.

SUMMARY

A. TYPES OF RATIOS

1. *Liquidity ratios:* used to measure the ability to meet maturing obligations in the near future.
2. *Leverage ratios:* used to evaluate the use of debt financing.
3. *Activity ratios:* used to evaluate the level of asset commitment and the efficiency of asset usage.
4. *Profitablity ratios:* used to evaluate the degree to which the activities of the company result in profits.

B. LIQUIDITY RATIOS

1. Current Ratio
   a. Use: a measure of the ability of the company to meet obligations in the near future.
   b. Formula: current assets ÷ current liabilities.

2. Acid Test Ratio
   a. Use: a measure of ability of the company to meet maturing obligations under conditions in which inventory could not be liquidated.
   b. Formula: (current assets − inventory) ÷ current liabilities.

C. LEVERAGE RATIOS

1. Debt Ratio
   a. Use: measure the percent of assets that are financed through debt.
   b. Formula: total debt ÷ total assets.
2. Times Interest Earned
   a. Use: indication of the ability to meet interest payments.
   b. Formula: (earnings before tax + interest) ÷ interest.

D. ACTIVITY RATIOS

1. Inventory turnover
   a. Use: measure of the efficiency of inventory usage.
   b. Formula: sales ÷ inventory.
2. Average Collection Period
   a. Use: measure of the average number of days between the sale of a product and receipt of payment. Provides a quick check on credit policy.
   b. Formula: 365 x (accounts receivable ÷ sales).
3. Fixed Asset Turnover
   a. Use: measure of the efficiency of fixed asset usage.
   b. Formula: sales ÷ fixed assets.
4. Total Asset Turnover
   a. Use: an overall indicator of the efficiency of asset usage.
   b. Formula: sales ÷ total assets.

E. PROFITABILITY RATIOS

1. Operating Profit Margin
   a. Use: measure of the ability to use sales to generate profits, before considering financing or taxes.
   b. Formula: net operating income ÷ sales.
2. Net Profit Margin
   a. Use: measure of the ability to convert sales to profit after tax.
   b. Formula: profit after tax ÷ sales.

3. Earning Power
   a. Use: measure of the ability to use assets to generate operating profits.
   b. Formula: net operating income ÷ total assets.
4. Return on Net Worth
   a. Use: measure of the return on the owners investment.
   b. Formula: net income ÷ net worth.

F. THE PROFITABILITY SYSTEM

The following chart shows the relationship between return on net worth and various other operating results measured by ratios discussed in this chapter.

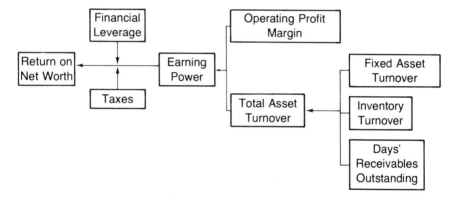

Return on net worth is a function of earning power, financial leverage, and taxes. Earning power, in turn, is a function of operating profit margin and total asset turnover. Total asset turnover is primarily affected by fixed asset turnover, inventory turnover, and days' receivables outstanding.

PROBLEM

Below are the financial statements for Bestway Electric Appliances.
a. Compute each of the ratios discussed in the chapter each year. Compare your answers to the solutions shown.
b. Compare the ratios for the two years with each other as well as with the industry average (given on page 22) to determine what caused the profits to be what they were.
c. What might the company do about this problem?

BESTWAY ELECTRIC APPLIANCES / Balance Sheets For:

	Dec. 31 1974	Dec. 31 1975		Dec. 31 1974	Dec. 31 1975
Cash	$ 80,000	$ 90,000	Accounts Payable	$ 50,000	$ 55,000
Accounts Receivable	170,000	190,000	Notes Payable	110,000	135,000
Inventory	200,000	220,000	Total Current		
Total Current Assets	450,000	500,000	Liabilities	160,000	190,000
Fixed Assets (net)	200,000	220,000	Long Term Debt	90,000	105,000
Total Assets	$650,000	$720,000	Stockholders Equity		
			Common Stock		
			($1 part)	100,000	100,000
			Paid-in Capital	100,000	100,000
			Retained Earnings	200,000	225,000
			Total Shareholders		
			Equity	400,000	425,000
			Total Liabilities		
			and Net Worth	$650,000	$720,000

BESTWAY ELECTRIC APPLIANCES / Income Statements for Years Ending:

		Dec. 31 1974		Dec. 31 1975
Sales		$900,000		$1,000,000
Cost of Goods Sold	$720,000		$808,000	
General & Admin. Exp.	80,000		90,000	
Depreciation	20,000		22,000	
Total Operating Exp.		820,000		920,000
Operating Profit		80,000		80,000
Interest		13,000		17,000
Earnings Before Taxes		67,000		63,000
Taxes		26,000		24,000
Net Profit		$ 41,000		$ 39,000
Earnings per Share		$0.41		$0.39

SOLUTION

a. Each of the ratios for each year can be computed as shown below.

BESTWAY ELECTRIC APPLIANCE

	1974	1975	Industry Average
LIQUIDITY RATIOS			
Current Ratio	2.8	2.6	2.5
Acid Test Ratio	1.6	1.5	1.3
LEVERAGE RATIOS			
Debt Ratio	.38	.41	.45
Times Interest Earned	6.2	4.7	7.5
ACTIVITY RATIOS			
Inventory Turnover	4.5	4.6	4.5
Average Collection Period	69 days	69 days	57 days
Fixed Asset Turnover	4.5	4.6	4.5
Total Asset Turnover	1.4	1.4	1.4
PROFITABILITY RATIOS			
Operating Profit Margin	8.9%	8.0%	9.3%
Net Profit Margin	4.6%	3.9%	4.9%
Earning Power	12.3%	11.1%	13.0%
Return on Net Worth	10.3%	9.2%	13.0%

b. Using the profitability system approach, you first observe that return on net worth and earning power were below the industry average in 1974 and fell further in 1975. Since the debt ratio increased, the average tax rate remained constant, and earning power decreased. The problem seems to lie in the operations of the company and not in financing or taxes. Total asset turnover is the same as the industry average for both years, but the operating profit margin is low for 1974 and lower for 1975. In summary, the level of asset usage appears to be satisfactory, but the *operating profit margin* is low and falling.

c. Without a more detailed look at the operations of the company it is not possbile to do more than speculate on what might be done to improve the operating profit margin. Several alternatives are, however, worthy of investigation. One possibility is that they have not adjusted their pricing structure to current market conditions and are therefore selling their product at an unrealistically low price. This could be corrected by merely readjusting their pricing structure. Another area to study would be the cost structure of their manufacturing operation. Standardization of parts, a decrease in the variety of products produced, and other methods of increasing efficiency are all possibilities. In summary, they must either raise the average price per unit or reduce the average production cost per unit if they are to improve the operating profit margin.

2

PRO-FORMA ANALYSIS

Pro-forma analysis consists of developing projected financial statements for future periods. It is a useful tool for predicting the financial results of various decisions and estimating funds requirements. Such analysis avoids later panic situations and allows the company to base decisions on careful reasoning rather than guesswork.

The first step in preparing pro-forma financial statements is to forecast sales. The sales forecast is vital because sales provide the primary source of revenues as well as having a major effect on most expense categories. The level of sales also has an important effect on the amount of assets required and on the level of current liabilities. Sales forecasts will not be discussed in detail here since a separate chapter would be required to do the topic justice. Also, this is a finance text and the financial manager seldom has the primary responsibility for the preparation of a sales forecast. Typically it is provided by other members of the management team. This chapter starts with a sales forecast and works forward to pro-forma income statements and balance sheets.

The preparation of pro-forma financial statements from a sales forecast consists of two main steps. The first step is to project or forecast certain items which will be part of the financial statements. Among the forecasted items are fixed costs, the relationship between variable costs and sales, the amount of each asset category required to support the forecasted sales level, the spontaneous current liabilities (such as accounts payable) to be generated by a particular level of sales, etc. These forecasted inputs are the information on which pro-forma financial statements are based. The second step is to use this information to develop pro-forma financial statements in a manner not totally unlike that used to prepare financial statements based on historical data.

In this chapter, the preparation of financial statements from the forecasted data will be treated first, followed by the forecasting of the necessary inputs and relationships. This approach gives you a better understanding of what information must be forecasted and how it will be used.

Upon completion of this chapter, you should be able to work from a sales forecast to develop projected financial statements for future periods. You should be able to use and modify these statements to test the effects of various possible outcomes and decisions on the financial position of the firm.

A. PRO-FORMA INCOME STATEMENTS

1. Pro-forma analysis consists of the preparation of estimated financial statements for future periods. Pro-forma analysis is used for such purposes as planning future funds needs and evaluating the effects of alternate strategies. The early sections of this chapter will deal with the mechanics of pro-forma analysis. The forecasting of the required inputs will be dealt with in the latter part of the chapter.

2. In preparing pro-forma analysis, the first step is normally the development of a pro-forma income statement. Allied Product's 1975 income statement is shown below. The blanks to the right are provided for the completion of a pro-forma income statement for 1976. Sales for 1976 are expected to be $200; fixed costs are expected to be $75; and variable costs are expected to be 50% of sales. Use the space below to compute the 1976 pro-forma income statement through net operating income.

ALLIED PRODUCTS COMPANY / Income Statements / Years Ending Dec. 31

	1975 Actual	1976 Pro-forma
Sales	$150	_____
Variable Costs	75	_____
Gross Profit	75	_____
Fixed Operating Costs	60	_____
Net Operating Income	$ 15	_____

Skip to Frame 5 if you got the correct answer.

---

2. 1976 pro-forma income statement

Sales	$200
Variable Costs	100
Gross Profit	100
Fixed Operating Costs	75
Net Operating Income	$ 25

3. Sales are, as stated, expected to be $200 for 1976. Variable costs are expected to be .50 x $200 = $_____ . Gross profit, therefore, is expected to be $200 − $100 = $_____ and net operating income is expected to be $100 − $75 = $_____ .

4. American Stores expects sales of $100 for 1976. Variable costs are expected to be 50% of sales and fixed costs are expected to be $20 a year. Compute the expected net operating income for 1976.

Sales	_____
Variable Costs	_____
Gross Profit	_____
Fixed Costs	_____
Net Operating Income	_____

5. Consolidated Stores will sell window air conditioning units during the coming season. The units cost the store $140 each. The fixed costs will be $20,000 for the season. In addition to the $140 purchase price, the only other variable cost per unit will be a $10 commission paid to the salesman. Management estimates that 1,000 units can be sold at a $200 retail price or 1,500 units can be sold at a $180 retail price. Compute the expected net operating income for each price level.

	$180 price	*$200 price*
Sales	$270,000	$200,000
Variable Costs	_____	_____
Gross Profit	_____	_____
Fixed Costs	_____	_____
Net Operating Income	_____	_____

Skip to Frame 7 if you got the correct answer.

---

3. $100
   100
   25

4.
Sales	$100
Variable Costs	50
Gross Profit	50
Fixed Costs	20
Net Operating Income	30

5. Net operating income at $180 price = $25,000
   Net operating income at $200 price = $30,000

6. Total variable cost per unit is the $140 purchase price plus the $10 sales commission, or $150. At the $180 price, total variable costs are $150 x 1,500 = $225,000 and gross profit is expected to be $270,000 - $225,000 = _____ . Fixed Cost is expected to be $20,000 and net operating income is expected to be $45,000 - $20,000 = _____ .

   At the $200 price, total variable cost is expected to be _____; gross profit is expected to be _____; and net operating income is expected to be _____ .

7. The next step in preparing a pro-forma income statement is the inclusion of debt service costs. Going back to Allied Products (Frame 2), compute the expected 1976 earnings before tax (EBT) based on an expected interest expense of $5.

	1975 Actual	1976 Pro-forma
Sales		
Net Operating Income	$15	_____
Interest	5	_____
Earning Before Tax	$10	_____

Skip to Frame 10 if you got the correct answer.

8. The expected net operating income for 1976 (from Frame 2) was $25. With an interest expense of $5, expected earnings before tax would be $25 - $5 = *$20*.

9. Consolidated Stores (Frame 5) expects interest expense of $10,000 in 1976. If they use the $200 per unit pricing policy, earnings before tax are expected to be _____ .

10. The next step is to compute expected taxes and net income. If Allied Products (Frame 7) faces a 50% tax rate on all income, taxes for 1976 are

---

6. $45,000
   $25,000
   $150,000
   $50,000
   $30,000

7. Earnings Before Tax = $25 - $5 = *$20*

9. Earnings Before Tax = $30,000 - $10,000 = *$20,000*

expected to be $_____ and net income is expected to be
$_____ .

Skip to Frame 12 if you got the correct answer.

11. Earnings before taxes were expected to be $20 for Allied Products. Taxes
of 50% would be $10 and net income would be:

Earnings Before Tax	$20
Tax	10
Net Income	$10

12. The final step in preparing pro-forma results of operations is to deduct
expected dividends from expected net income to arrive at the expected
increase in retained earnings. Allied Products will distribute 40% of net
income in the form of dividends, with the remainder going to retained
earnings for 1976. Expected dividends = $_____ . Expected
increase in retained earnings = $_____ .

13. You have now completed, in steps, the pro-forma income statement for
Allied Products for the year 1976. Summarize the results obtained thus far
in the space provided below.

ALLIED PRODUCT COMPANY / Income Statements / Years Ending Dec. 31

	1975 (actual)	1976 (pro-forma)
Sales	$150	_____
Variable Costs	75	_____
Gross Profit	75	_____
Fixed Operating Costs	60	_____
Net Operating Income	15	_____
Interest	5	_____
Earnings Before Tax	10	_____
Tax	5	_____
Net Income	$ 5	_____
Dividends	2	_____
Increase in Retained Earnings	$ 3	_____

---

10. $10
    $10

12. $4
    $10 - $4 = *$6*

13. Sales = $200; Variable Costs = $100; Gross Profit = $100; Fixed
    Operating Costs = $75; Net Operating Income = $25; Interest = $5;
    Earnings Before Tax = $20; Tax = $10; Net Income = $10; Dividends
    = $4; Increase in Retained Earnings = $6.

14. If you are familiar with the preparation of financial statements based on historical data, you will note that the technique is essentially the same for pro-forma statements. The primary difference is that pro-forma statements are usually presented in less detail because the forecasts are not as accurate as the historical data. Such detail based on forecasts would be a waste of time.

15. As a reinforcing exercise, prepare a pro-forma income statement for Southeast Carryout for 1976. Sales are expected to be $100,000 and cost of goods sold is expected to be 60% of sales. Rent and utilities are expected to total $500 a month. Labor is expected to total $1,500 a month, and advertising expenses will be $2,000 for the year. Miscellaneous expenses, not included in the above categories, are expected to total $3,000 for the year. The company expects to have average debt outstanding of $40,000 with an interest rate of 6% per year. No dividends will be paid. Southeast Carryout pays income tax averaging 30% of earnings before tax.

SOUTHEAST CARRYOUT / Pro-forma Income Statement / Year Ending Dec. 31, 1976

Sales   _____
Cost of Goods Sold   _____
Gross Profit   _____
  Labor Expense   _____
  Rent and Utilities   _____
  Advertising   _____
  Miscellaneous Expense   _____
Net Operating Income   _____
Interest   _____
Earnings Before Tax   _____
Tax   _____
Net Income   _____
Dividends   _____
Increase in Retained Earnings   _____
                                               _____

The answer appears in Frame 16.

16.

Sales		$100,000
Cost of Goods Sold (.60 x $100,000)		60,000
Gross Profit (100,000 - 60,000)		40,000
Labor Expense (12 x $1,500)	$18,000	
Rent and Utilities (12 x $500)	6,000	
Advertising	2,000	
Miscellaneous Expense	3,000	29,000
Net Operating Income		11,000
Interest ($40,000 x .06)		2,400
Earnings Before Tax		8,600
Tax ($8,600 x .30)		2,580
Net Income ($8600 - $2,580)		$6,020
Dividends		0
Increase in Retained Earnings		$6,020

Skip to Frame 19 if you got the correct answer.

17. Suppose that Southeast Carryout achieves a sales level of $120,000 instead of $100,000 by spending an additional $2,000 on advertising. All other information given in Frame 15 remains unchanged. Prepare another pro-forma income statement to show the effect of this increase in sales.

The answer appears in Frame 18.

18. The new pro-forma income statement would appear as follows:

Sales		$120,000
Cost of Goods Sold (.6 x $120,000)		72,000
Gross Profit ($120,000 - $72,000)		48,000
Labor Expense (12 x $1,500)	$18,000	
Rent and Utilities (12 x $500)	6,000	
Advertising ($2,000 + $2,000)	4,000	
Miscellaneous Expense	3,000	31,000
Net Operating Income ($48,000 - $31,000)		17,000
Interest ($40,000 x .06)		2,400
Earnings Before Tax		14,600
Tax (.3 x $14,600)		4,380
Net Income		$10,220
Dividends		0
Increase in Retained Earnings		$10,220

19. This completes the introduction to the preparation of pro-forma income statements. The next step is to find out what funds will be required to support this level of activity.

B. PRO-FORMA BALANCE SHEETS

20. The pro-forma income statement helped to project the profit results of operations for a future period. The pro-forma balance sheet helps to convert these figures to an estimate of funds needed and available. As with pro-forma income statements, this section deals with the mechanics of pro-forma statement preparation. The forecasting of the required inputs will be dealt with later.

21. To begin the preparation of a pro-forma balance sheet, it is necessary to develop some estimate of the relationships between level of business activity and level of assets and liabilities. For the initial illustration, assume that current assets and current liabilities remain at fixed percentages of sales and that the future level of fixed assets is known. This is a justifiable set of assumptions for pro-forma analysis. The primary justification for the assumptions concerning current assets and current liabilities is that these accounts do fluctuate with the level of activity. Fixed assets, on the other hand, are the result of specific decisions made some time in advance of acquisition. They are, therefore, normally forecast based on existing expansion plans.

22. Refer to the pro-forma 1976 income statement for Allied Products Company in Frame 13. You will now work toward the preparation of a pro-forma balance sheet. Below is the balance sheet for December 31, 1975.

ALLIED PRODUCTS COMPANY / Balance Sheet / December 31, 1975

Current Assets	$120	Current Liabilities	$ 30
Fixed Assets (net		Long Term Debt (10%)	50
of depreciation)	80	Common Stock	40
Total Assets	$200	Retained Earnings	80
		Total Liabilities and	
		Net Worth	$200

23. The first step is to estimate the asset level for 1976. Plant expansion plans call for a fixed asset level of $100 by the end of 1976. The ratio of current assets to sales is expected to remain the same as in 1975. Current assets at the end of 1975 were 120/150 = _____% of sales. If they continue at the same proportion of sales for 1976, current assets will grow to .80 x $200 = $_____ . Projected total assets for the end of 1976 are therefore $100 + $160 = $_____ .

---

23. 80%
$160
$260

24. The ratio of current liabilities to sales is also expected to be the same in 1976 as in 1975. The ratio of current liabilities to sales was 30/150 = _____% at the end of 1975. If this ratio continues, current liabilities will be .20 x $200 = $_____ . No changes in long term debt or common stock are anticipated. The 1976 pro-forma income statement shows that a $_____ increase in retained earnings is expected. The total level of retained earnings, therefore, is projected to be $80 + $6 = $_____ . Summing up, total liabilities and net worth are projected to be $40 + $50 + $40 + $86 = $_____ .

25. In Frame 23, total assets were projected to be $_____ and in Frame 24 total liabilities and net worth were projected to be $_____ . The $44 excess of projected total assets over projected total liabilities and net worth indicates that projected funding will *not* be sufficient to meet the projected asset needs. Allied Products will need $44 in additional funding to meet projected 1976 needs. The need can be met by borrowing, selling additional stock, or acquiring fewer assets.

26. Use the space below to summarize the projected 1976 balance sheet.

ALLIED PRODUCTS COMPANY / Balance Sheet / December 31

	1975(actual)	1976(pro-forma)
Current Assets	$120	_____
Fixed Assets (net of depreciation)	80	_____
Total Assets	$200	_____
Current Liabilities	$ 30	_____
Long Term Debt (10% interest)	50	_____
Common Stock	40	_____
Retained Earnings	80	_____
Total Liabilities and Net Worth	$200	_____
Additional Funds Needed		_____

---

24. 20%
$40
$6
$86
$216

25. $260
$216

26. Current Assets = $160; Fixed Assets = $100; Total Assets = $260; Current Liabilities = $40; Long Term Debt = $50; Common Stock = $40; Retained Earnings = $86; Total Liabilities and Net Worth = $216; Additional Funds Needed = $44.

27. Allied Products (Frames 13 and 26) is considering a change in credit policy which would decrease accounts receivable and therefore increase turnover of current assets to 2. Prepare a pro-forma 1976 balance sheet based on the new credit policy.

ALLIED PRODUCTS COMPANY / Pro-forma Balance Sheet / December 31, 1975

Current Assets	_____	Current Liabilities	_____
Fixed Assets		Long Term Debt (104)	_____
(net of depreciation)	_____	Common Stock	_____
Total Assets	===========	Retained Earnings	_____
		Total Liabilities	
		and Net Worth	===========

The new credit policy is expected to result in excess funds of _____ at the end of 1976.

Skip to Frame 30 if you got the correct answer.

28. The answer to Frame 27 is computed as follows:
    a. Current Assets = sales ÷ current asset turnover
    $$= \$200 \div 2$$
    $$= \$100$$
    b. Total Assets = $100 + $100 = *$200*
    c. Additional funds needed = $200 - $216 = (*$16*)
    d. The new credit policy is expected to result in excess funds of *$16* (Total Liabilities and Net Worth indicate total anticipated sources of funds while Total Assets indicate anticipated uses. If anticipated sources exceed anticipated uses, excess funds are expected.)

29. Go back to the pro-forma balance sheet in Frame 26. (Ignore the possible change considered in Frame 27.) Allied Products decides it is possible to decrease the current ratio to 2:1 by holding current assets at the anticipated $160 level and increasing current liabilities. What would be the additional funds needed if this plan were implemented?

---

27. Expected excess funds at the end of 1975 are $16.

29. Total assets will remain unchanged at $260. Current liabilities will increase to $80. Total liabilities $ net worth will increase to $256. The addtional funds needed = $260 - $256 = $4.

30. Pro-forma analysis will now be used to gauge a company's degree of risk exposure. IHT Corporation is interested in the riskiness of its capital structure, and wants to know if it could meet its debt obligations in the face of a 20% sales decline. The company has a debt payment of $200 due each year. Long term debt will be $2,000 at the end of 1976 and interest expense will be $168 for 1976. In preparation for the analysis, the following estimates have been made.

a. The cost of goods sold would remain the same percent of sales, and fixed operating expenses would remain constant at $3,000.

b. Tax would continue to equal 50% of the earnings before tax and no dividends would be paid if a sales decline of this magnitude occurred.

c. The cash balance could be safely reduced by only 10%.

d. Accounts receivable turnover would decrease to 5-1/3.

e. It would not be possible to decrease inventory in the face of declining sales. The best that could be done would be to hold inventory constant and avoid stockpiling.

f. Fixed assets could be reduced to $3,900 by not replacing certain equipment as it wore out.

g. Current liabilities would have to be reduced by 10%.

Based on this information and the existing financial statements, prepare a pro-forma income statement for 1976 based on a 20% sales decline.

IHT CORPORATION / Income Statement / Year Ending Dec. 31

	1975(actual)	1976(pro-forma)
Sales	$10,000	$8,000
Cost of Goods Sold	6,000	_____
Gross Profit	4,000	_____
Fixed Operating Costs	3,000	_____
Net Operating Income	1,000	_____
Interest	184	_____
Earnings Before Tax	816	_____
Tax	408	_____
Net Income	$ 408	_____
Dividends	$ 204	_____
Increase in Retained Earnings	$204	_____

---

30. Net Income = $16; Dividends = $0; Increase in Retained Earnings = $16.

31. The 1976 pro-forma income statement should have appeared as follows:

IHT CORPORATION / Income Statement / Year Ending Dec. 31, 1976

Sales (given)	$8,000
Cost of Goods Sold (.60 x $8,000)	4,800
Gross Profit	3,200
Fixed Operating Expenses (given)	3,000
Net Operating Income	200
Interest (given)	168
Earnings Before Tax	32
Tax (.50 x $32)	16
Net Income	16
Dividends (given)	0
Increase in Retained Earnings ($16 - $0)	$ 16

32. Prepare a pro-forma 1976 income statement for IHT Corporation based on a 10% decline in sales and no dividends. All other information given in Frame 30 remains the same.

IHT CORPORATION / Income Statement / Year Ending Dec. 31

	1975(actual)	1976(pro-forma)
Sales	$10,000	$9,000
Cost of Goods Sold	6,000	_____
Gross Profit	4,000	_____
Fixed Operating Expenses	3,000	_____
Net Operating Income	1,000	_____
Interest	184	_____
Earnings Before Tax	816	_____
Tax	408	_____
Net Income	$ 408	$ _____
Dividends	204	_____
Increase in Retained Earnings	$ 204	$ _____

If you had difficulty with this problem, review Frames 1 to 17 before continuing.

33. Based on a 20% decline in sales and the information given in Frame 30, prepare a pro-forma 1976 balance sheet for IHT.

---

32. Net Income = *$216*; Dividends = *$0*; Increase in Retained Earnings = *$216.*

IHT CORPORATION / Balance Sheets / December 31

	1975(actual)	1976(pro-forma)
Cash	$ 200	_____
Accounts Receivable	1,800	_____
Inventory	2,000	_____
Total Current Assets	4,000	_____
Fixed Assets (net of depreciation)	4,000	_____
Total Assets	$8,000	_____
Current Liabilities	$2,000	_____
Long Term Debt (8%)	2,200	_____
Common Stock	2,000	_____
Retained Earnings	1,800	_____
Total Liabilities and Net Worth	$8,000	_____
Additional Funds Needed (Excess Funds)		_____

Skip to Frame 36 if you got the correct answer.

34. The answer to Frame 33 is computed as follows:
Cash = $200 - .10($200) = *$180*
Accounts Receivable = 8,000/ (5 1/3) = $8,000/(16/3) = $8,000(3/16) = *$1,500*
Inventory (no change) = *$2,000*
Fixed Assets (given) = *$3,900*
Total Assets = *$7,580*
Current Liabilities = $2,000 - .10($2,000) = *$1,800*
Long Term Debt (given) = *$2,000*
Common Stock (no change) = *$2,000*
Retained Earnings = $1,800 + $16 = *$1,816*
Total Liabilities and Net Worth = *$7,616*
Additional Funds Needed (Excess Funds) = $7,580 - $7,616 = *($36)*
A 20% decline in sales would leave IHT with $36 in excess funds at the end of 1976. No additional borrowing would be needed.

35. A 10% decline in sales for 1976 would be expected to lead to a net income of $216 and an increase in retained earnings of $216. Based on the

---

33. Total Assets = *$7,580*; Total Liabilities and Net Worth = *$7,616*; Additional Funds Needed (Excess Funds) = $36.
The company could experience a 20% decline in sales in 1976 and still have sufficient funds available.

following estimates, prepare a pro-forma balance sheet for 1976 based on a 10% sales decline.

a. The cash balance could be safely reduced by only 5%.

b. Accounts receivable would be $1,600.

c. Inventory would remain the same as in 1975.

d. Fixed assets would remain the same as in 1975.

e. Current liabilities would have to be rescued by 5%.

IHT CORPORATION / Pro-forma Balance Sheet / December 31, 1976

Cash	_____	Current Liabilities	_____
Accounts Receivable	_____	Long Term Debt (8%)	_____
Inventory	_____	Common Stock	_____
Total Current Liabilities	_____	Retained Earnings	_____
Fixed Assets	_____	Total Liabilities	
Total Assets	========	and Net Worth	========
		(Excess Funds)	========

36. IHT can expect to be able to meet its 1976 debt payments in the face of a 20% decline in sales. The company is, however, interested in what would happen if sales remained at this lower level for an additional year. Would IHT be able to meet an additional $200 scheduled debt repayment in 1977? The following information was developed in preparation for this analysis.

a. All income statement items down to interest will remain the same as for 1976. Interest will decline to $152.

b. Cash and accounts receivable could not be reduced further.

c. Inventory could be reduced 10% by the end of 1977.

d. Fixed assets could not be reduced below $3,900.

e. It would be necessary to reduce current liabilities to the same percent of sales that existed in 1975.

Space for analysis is provided on page 37.

IHT would be able to experience a one year sales decline of 20% without running into financial difficulty. However, if sales remained at the lower level through 1977, $140 in additional funds would be needed.

35. Cash = $190; Accounts Receivable = $1,600; Inventory = $2,000; Fixed Assets = $4,000; Total Assets = $7,790; Current Liabilities = $1,900; Long Term debt = $2,000; Common Stock = $2,000; Retained Earnings = $2,016; Total Liabilities and Net Worth = $7,916. Additional Funds Needed (Excess Funds) = $216.

IHT CORPORATION / Income Statement / Year Ending Dec. 31

	1975(actual)	1976(pro-forma)	1977(pro-forma)
Sales	$10,000	$8,000	_____
Cost of Goods Sold	6,000	4,800	_____
Gross Profit	4,000	3,200	_____
Fixed Operating Expenses	3,000	3,000	_____
Net Operating Income	1,000	200	_____
Interest	184	168	_____
Earnings Before Tax	816	32	_____
Tax	408	16	_____
Net Income	408	16	_____
Dividends	$ 204	0	_____
Increase in Retained Earnings	$ 204	$ 16	_____

IHT CORPORATION / Balance Sheet / December 31

	1975 (actual)	1976 (pro-forma)	1977 (pro-forma)
Cash	$ 200	$ 180	_____
Accounts Receivable	1,800	1,500	_____
Inventory	2,000	2,000	_____
Total Current Assets	4,000	3,680	_____
Fixed Assets (net of depreciation)	4,000	3,900	_____
Total Assets	$8,000	$7,580	_____
Current Liabilities	$2,000	$1,800	_____
Long Term Debt	2,200	2,000	_____
Common Stock	2,000	2,000	_____
Retained Earnings	1,800	1,816	_____
Total Liabilities & Net Worth	$8,000	$7,616	_____
Additionals Funds Needed (Excess Funds)		(36)	_____

---

36. Net Operating Income = $200; Interest = $152; Earnings Before Tax = $48; Tax = $24; Net Income = $24; Dividends = $0; Increase in Retained Earnings = $24; Cash = $180; Accounts Receivable = $1,500; Inventory = $1,800; Fixed Assets = $3,900; Total Assets = $7,380; Current Liabilities = $1,600; Long Term Debt = $1,800; Common Stock = $2,000; Retained Earning = $1,840; Total Liabilities & Net Worth = $7,240; Additional Funds Needed = *$140*.

C. FORECASTING FINANCIAL RESULTS

37. Pro-forma financial statements are summary results of many forecasts. The most important forecast is normally the sales forecast. This is the forecast of the level of activity, and most other financial forecasts of the firm follow from it. The financial manager is seldom the person with primary responsibility for the sales forecast, and the development of a sales forecast is beyond the scope of this book. The available space will be devoted to an introduction to some of the major methods of forecasting other financial variables from the sales forecast. The reader who is interested in the development of sales forecasts or is interested in pursuing other forecasting problems in more detail is referred to one of the many texts available on the topic of forecasting.

38. Once a sales forecast has been developed, the effect of sales on numerous other factors must be evaluated. Fixed costs must be estimated and the ratio of variable costs to sales must be forecasted. The effect of the projected sales level on each asset and liability account must be estimated. This section will be devoted to an analysis of various ways to forecast these relationships.

39. To illustrate the various methods of forecasting, the relationship between the cost of goods sold (CGS) and sales will be used. The sales and CGS data for Exotic Product Company appear below.

Year	1972	1973	1974	1975	1976 (forecasted)
Sales	$100	$110	$130	$150	$170
Cost of Goods Sold	65	66	72	75	
CGS/Sales	65%	60%	55.4%	50%	

The simplest forecast would be no change from the previous year, or an estimated cost of goods sold of $_____ for 1976. However, it would be naive to think that the cost of goods sold is not related to sales. On the other hand, it may be reasonable to expect little change in certain fixed cost categories such as depreciation.

40. One simple approach is to assume that the financial variable will remain the same percent of sales as in the previous year. If this method were used, the cost of goods sold forecast for 1976 would be $_____ .

---

39. $75

40. .50 x $170 = *$85*

Skip to Frame 42 if you got the correct answer.

41. If you had used this method to forecast cost of goods sold for 1974, your forecast would have been $_____$, and your forecast would have been off by $78 - $72 = $_____$.

42. There is a certain danger in assuming that the CGS/Sales figure for 1975 is more representative than the figures for other years. You will note that CGS/Sales *does / does not* change from year to year. Therefore, it might be worthwhile to analyze the trend in this ratio. Use the graph space provided below to plot this relationship.

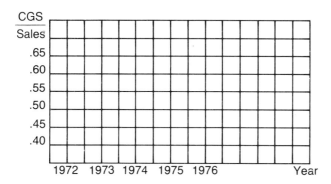

The answer appears in Frame 43.

43. You should have plotted the ratio as shown below.

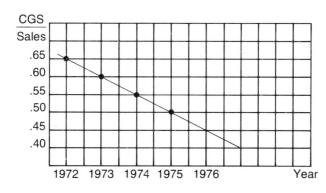

---

41. .60 x $130 = *$78*
$6

42. does

The analysis of this trend requires a certain amount of judgment, so different analysts might reach somewhat different conclusions. However, it would appear that the CGS/Sales for 1976 would be approximately _____% if the trend in this ratio continues. Therefore, 1976 cost of goods sold would be forecasted as .45 x $170 = $_____.

44. Another approach would be to study the relationship between sales levels and the cost of goods sold through correlation analysis. The simplest approach to correlation analysis is the scatter diagram method. Use the following graph space to plot the cost of goods sold against sales for Exotic Product Company. Fit a straight line to your observations.

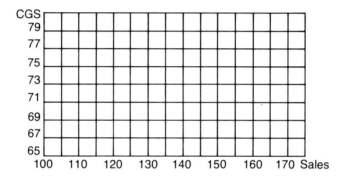

The correct analysis appears in Frame 45.

45. The straight line should have been fit to the observations as follows:

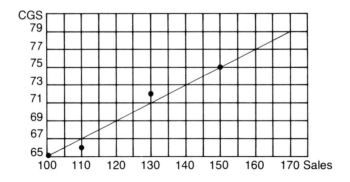

---

44. 45%
    76.5

This line can now be used to forecast the cost of goods sold for 1976. Since sales for 1976 are expected to be $170, cost of goods sold is therefore forecast to be $_____ .

46. Unfortunately, a different forecast was reached with each method of forecasting. In Frame 39, a 1976 cost of goods sold of $_____ was forecast based on the assumption of no change. In Frame 40, the 1976 cost of goods sold was forecast as $_____ by assuming that the ratio of cost of goods sold to sales would remain the same as in 1975. In Frame 43, the changes in CGS/Sales over time were analyzed, and 1976 cost of goods sold was forecast to be $_____ . In Frames 44 and 45, the relationship between the level of sales and the cost of goods sold was analyzed, and the cost of goods sold for 1976 was forecast to be $_____ . How do you forecast when each forecasting method yields different results? The answer to this question is that you must choose the forecasting method which is most appropriate for each forecast. Following another exercise in forecasting techniques, the selection of the appropriate forecasting method will be discussed.

47. International Controls has the sales and cost of goods sold experience shown below. Prepare a 1976 cost of goods sold forecast based on the analysis of CGS/Sales over time and based on the relationship between the level of sales and cost of goods sold. (Note - a precise answer cannot be achieved.)

Year	1971	1972	1973	1974	1975	1976 (forecasted)
Sales	$100	$100	$110	$120	$120	$130
Cost of Goods Sold	60	61	66	70	68	
CGS/Sales	60%	61%	60%	58.3%	56.7%	

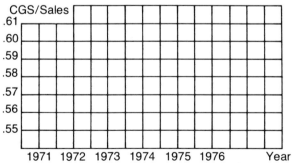

45. $79

46. $75; $85; $76.50; $79

A reasonable estimate of the CGS/Sales for 1976 is _____%. Based on this ratio, the forecasted cost of goods sold for 1976 is $_____ .

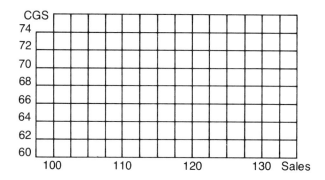

Based on the analysis of the relationship between sales level and cost of goods sold, it would appear that a reasonable estimate of the cost of goods for 1976 is $_____ .

The answer appears in Frame 48.

48. It is seldom possible to come up with a precise forecast in the same manner that you can develop a precise answer if asked to compute the square root of 9. Forecasting is part science and part art. From the graph shown below, it appears that a CGS/Sales of a little over 55% might be a reasonable forecast for 1976. For example, a CGS/Sales of 55.5% would yield a cost of goods sold equal to $72.15.

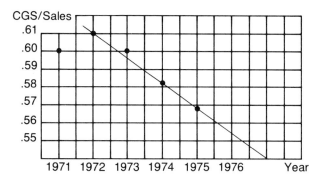

Based on the relationship between the sales level and cost of goods sold, it appears that $73.00 would be a reasonable estimate of the cost of goods sold for 1976.

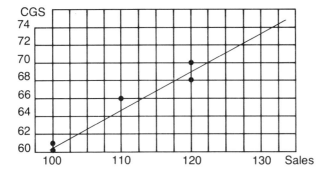

49. As noted earlier, forecasts vary, depending on which forecasting method is used. The choice of a forecasting method is therefore of some importance. The general guideline is to use your judgement in selecting a forecasting method dependent on the factors most likely to affect a particular financial variable. The application of this guideline to the forecasting of the cost of goods sold is somewhat difficult. First, it is reasonable to assume that the cost of goods sold consists of some fixed costs and some variable costs. Therefore, it would not be reasonable to expect the CGS/Sales ratio to remain constant at all sales levels. For this reason, the relationship between the sales level and the cost of goods sold is appropriate for study. However, there may be factors besides the sales level which cause CGS/Sales ratio to change over time. This would seem particularly important if changes in CGS/Sales were observed in the absence of changes in the level of sales. In the case of International Controls (Frames 47 and 48), the analyst would probably forecast a cost of goods sold figure between the two estimates.

50. Some expense items, such as rent, advertising, and depreciation, may be known in advance and require no forecasting effort. Others are usually made up of fixed portions and portions that are affected by the sales level. By studying the correlation of these items with sales and looking at the trend in their absolute values over time, an estimate of values for future periods can be determined. Interest payments, of course, depend on current debt and planned borrowing. It will be necessary to look at the pro-forma balance sheet to determine what additional borrowing is needed.

51. The accounts receivable level would generally be forecast by looking at the trend in the ratio of accounts receivable to sales over time. This would normally be the best predictor because accounts receivable are generated

by sales, but collection experience changes over time. The ratio of
inventory to sales, on the other hand, would normally be expected to
decrease as the sales level increases. The reason for this decrease is that the
company cannot operate at all without a certain base inventory. Beyond
this basic inventory, the level of inventory would not need to be increased
proportionately with sales. Analysis of the correlation between the sales
and inventory level would generally be most appropriate for forecasting
inventory.

52. For periods such as a year, the level of fixed assets can be determined
largely by studying existing plans for capital expenditures. For longer
periods, an analysis similar to that applied to inventory is generally most
appropriate.

53. The level of accounts payable can generally be forecast in the same manner
as accounts receivable. Accounts payable are someone else's accounts
receivable so the analysis is the same. The other current liabilities, except
short term debt, would generally need to be evaluated with reference to
both time and the sales level as was done with cost of goods sold.

54. Debt and equity are the result of policy decisions in response to projected
funds needs. These items, therefore, are estimated based on the anticipated
management response to the projected funds needs.

55. The approaches to forecasting financial relationships presented here are
relatively simple but quite useful. While more advanced methods, such as
multiple regression and exponential smoothing, are available, no
forecasting method is so sophisticated as to eliminate the need for
judgment and discretion in the development of forecasts. It is the
responsibility of the analyst to consider all factors of which he is aware in
preparing a forecast. Many considerations, such as the effect of the
appointment of a new credit manager, cannot be fit neatly into any purely
quantitative forecasting model. The art of successful forecasting consists of
the proper balance between those things which can and cannot be
quantified.

SUMMARY

A. PURPOSES OF PRO-FORMA ANALYSIS
1. Estimate future funds needs and availability.
2. Estimate the effects of various possible future events.
3. Study the effects of various strategies on the future financial position
   of the firm.

B. STEPS IN PRO-FORMA ANALYSIS

1. Forecast sales.
2. Forecast operating expenses based on the sales projection.
3. Forecast interest payments based on the existing level of debt adjusted for planned borrowing or repayment.
4. Forecast taxes and dividends based on the projected income level.
5. Estimate current asset levels necessary to support the forecasted sales.
6. Forecast the fixed asset level based on the sales forecast and existing plans for asset acquisition.
7. Estimate the current liability level that would be generated by the forecasted sales level.
8. Forecast long term debt based on existing debt and existing plans for borrowing or repayment.
9. Forecast equity based on existing equity, any anticipated increase or decrease in retained earnings, and any existing plans for issuing or retiring stock.
10. Compare total assets to total liabilities and net worth.
    a. If projected total assets exceed projected total liabilities and net worth, the difference between the two represents additional funds needed.
    b. If projected total assets are less than projected total liabilities and net worth, the difference between the two represents anticipated excess funds.

C. METHODS OF FORECASTING FINANCIAL RELATIONSHIPS

1. Unchanging items
   Some items, such as a long term lease payment, remain constant from year to year. For these items, next year's forecasted value equals last year's actual value.
2. Constant proportion of sales
   Some items remain a relatively constant proportion of sales. For these items, last year's proportion is applied to next year's forecasted sales.
3. Correlation with the sales level
   Many financial variables are related to sales but do not remain the same percent of sales at all sales levels. These relationships can frequently be evaluated using a scatter diagram with the financial variable on one axis and the sales level on the other.
4. Analysis over time
   Many variables show a definite trend over time, either in relationship to sales or independently. These items can be studied using a scatter diagram with the financial variable or its proportion of sales represented on one axis and time represented on the other axis.

5. Subjective evaluation
   Forecasting is never a purely mathematical exercise. The analyst must use his judgment in considering all relevant information, both quantitative and qualitative, of which he is aware.

PROBLEMS

PROBLEM 1:

Refer to the financial statements for Office Supply Corporation presented in Chapter 1. Office Supply wishes to prepare pro-forma financial statements for 1976. A sales forecast of $140 has been prepared. The company has no plans for additional borrowing, debt repayment, stock issue, or stock retirement at this time. All net income will be paid out in the form of dividends. A compensating balance requirement sets minimum cash needs at $10. A new credit manager has been hired, and he feels that he can increase accounts receivable turnover to 4 by the end of the year without losing sales. An investigation of changes in inventory reveals that the decreased turnover in 1975 was caused by expansion of product lines. They estimate that in addition to the existing stock, inventory equal to 20% of any sales over $120 will be required. Fixed asset turnover is

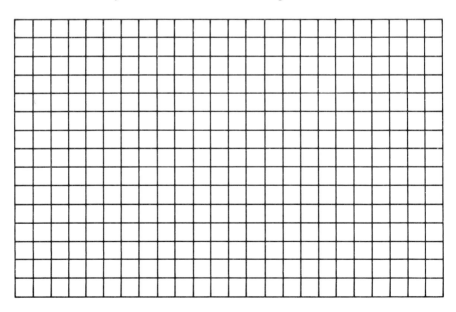

expected to follow the trend of the last several years. Sales for 1970, 1971, and 1972 were $60, $70, and $75, respectively. Current liabilities for 1970, 1971, and 1972 were $15, $18, and $20, respectively. Administrative overhead expenses for 1970, 1971, and 1972 were $18, $21, and $22.50, respectively. Graph space is provided on page 46 for your use in preparing forecasts.

PROBLEM 2:

Joyce Brown was employed part-time in a furniture store during her four years of college and has been employed full time with the same store for the two years since graduation. She feels that she has sufficient education in business administration and experience in furniture retailing to consider opening her own store. While she has little capital of her own, she has an uncle who is interested in her plans and may be willing to invest in such an enterprise. As part of her financial planning, she is interested in determining her needs for long term financing. She has decided that a reasonable approach is to forecast her total assets and current liabilities at the end of one year's operation. The difference between the two must be financed from long term sources. She expects to just break even on sales of $100,000 during the first year. She intends to lease a store but fixtures, etc, will require a fixed asset investment of $10,000. A minimum cash balance of $5,000 is felt to be prudent. In preparation for her analysis, she referred to *Key Business Ratios* by Dunn and Bradstreet for the following median ratios for furniture stores:

Ratio	D & B Median
Average Collection Period	97 days
Net Sales to Inventory	4.8
Current Ratio	2.76

Forecast net total assets, current liabilities, required long term financing, total liabilities, and net worth.

PROBLEM 3:

Ms. Brown (see Problem 2) also wishes to determine what proportion of her long term financing should be in the form of debt and what proportion should be in equity. She again referred to *Key Business Ratios* and noted that the median total debt to net worth ratio for furniture retailers was 96.9%.

SOLUTIONS

SOLUTION 1:

OFFICE SUPPLY CORPORATION
Pro-forma Income Statement / Year Ending December 31, 1976

Sales	$140
Cost of Goods Sold	70
Gross Profit	70
Administrative and Overhead Expense	42
Net Operating Income	28
Interest	6
Earnings Before Tax	22
Tax	11
Net Income	$ 11

OFFICE SUPPLY CORPORATION / Pro-forma Balance Sheet / December 31, 1976

ASSETS		LIABILITIES AND NET WORTH	
Cash	$ 10	Accounts Payable	$ 25
Accounts Receivable	35	Miscellaneous Accruals	25
Inventory	34	Total Current Liabilities	50
Current Assets	79	Long Term Debt	60
Fixed Assets	70	Common Stock	10
Total Assets	$149	Paid in Capital	10
		Retained Earnings	30
		Total Liabilities and Net Worth	$160
Additional Funds Needed (Excess Funds)			($11)

The following analysis was used in preparing this answer:

Year	1970	1971	1972	1973	1974	1975
Sales	$60	$70	$75	$80	$100	$120
Admin. & Op. Exp ÷ Sales	.30	.30	.30	.31	.30	.30
Current Liabilities ÷ Sales	.25	.257	.267	.25	.30	.333
Cost of Goods Sold ÷ Sales				.50	.50	.50
Fixed Assets ÷ Sales				.50	.50	.50

Interest: Based on statement that no change in debt is expected
Cash: Based on $10 compensating balance requirement
Accounts Receivable: $140 ÷ 4 = $35
Inventory: $30 + .20($140 − $120) = $34
Fixed Assets: .50 x $140 = $70
Total Current Liabilities: This is the most difficult item to forecast in this problem, and no two people are expected to get exactly the same answer.

The $50 estimate is based on the observed trend in current liabilities ÷ sales over recent years. A ratio of .35 or .36 seems reasonable for 1976. Fifty dollars is about midway between these two.

SOLUTION 2:

Sales (given)	$100,000
Cash (given)	5,000
Accounts Receivable (97/365) x $100,000	26,575
Inventory $100,000/4.8	20,833
Total Current Assets	52,408
Fixed Assets (given)	10,000
Total Assets	$62,408
Current Liabilities $52,408/2.76	18,988
Required Long Term Financing $62,408 − $18,988	$43,420
Total Liabilities and Net Worth	$62,408

SOLUTION 3:

Net Worth + Total Debt (Liabilities) = Total Liabilities & Net Worth
Net Worth + .969 x Net Worth   = $62,408
        1.969 x Net Worth   = $62,408
               Net Worth   = $31,695

Total Debt = $62,408 − $31,695 = $30,713
Long Term Debt = Total Debt − Current Liabilities
Long Term Debt = $30,713 − $18,988 = $11,725

The right hand side of the balance sheet should then appear as follows:

Current Liabilities	$18,988
Long Term Debt	11,725
Owner's Equity	31,695
Total Liabilities and Net Worth	$62,408

3
LEVERAGE

Through the varying of production and financing methods, companies can alter both the potential returns and the risks to which they are exposed. This chapter deals with the methods of evaluating the effects of changes in production and financing methods.

The particular production changes we are interested in involve tradeoffs between fixed and variable costs. *Fixed costs* are those that remain the same regardless of the level of production. Examples of fixed costs are lighting expense and building depreciation. *Variable costs* are those that change with the level of production. Examples are raw material and direct labor. The substitution of fixed operating costs for variable operating costs is called *operating leverage*.

The financial arrangements we are interested in involve substituting fixed-cost sources of funds, such as debt, for residual owner's equity. The use of fixed cost sources is called *financial leverage*.

In this chapter you learn how to evaluate the effects of fixed operating costs and fixed-cost sources of funds on potential returns, risk exposure, and the level of sales necessary for the company to break even.

A. OPERATING LEVERAGE

1. Operating leverage is used with the hope of increasing profits by reducing total costs. It also increases risk by committing the company to costs that must be met even if sales fall far below the level expected.

2. It is virtually impossible to think of a company that uses no operating leverage. This would imply *no* fixed costs. Therefore, the choice is not

whether or not to use operating leverage, but between more or less
_____ _____ .

3. ABC Corporation's only product is sold for $10 a unit. The company has fixed operating costs of $500 a year and variable costs of $5 a unit. If the company produces and sells 200 units a year, it will have sales of $10 x $200 = $_____ , total variable costs of $5 x 200 = $_____, gross profit of $2,000 - $1,000 = $_____ , and net operating income of $1,000 - $500 = $_____ .

The answer appears in Frame 4.

4. The answer to Frame 3 is as follows:

Sales ($10 x 200)	$2,000
Total variable costs ($5 x 200)	1,000
Gross profit	1,000
Fixed operating costs	500
Net operating income	$ 500

5. Horizon Corporation, one of ABC Corporation's competitors, uses a different production method. For Horizon, fixed operating costs are $600 a year, but variable costs are only $4 a unit. If Horizons sells 200 units at $10 each, total variable costs will be $_____ , gross profit will be $_____ , and net operating income will be $_____ .

Skip to Frame 7 if you got the correct answer.

6. The answer to Frame 5 is as follows:

Sales ($10 x 200)	$2,000
Total variable costs ($4 x 200)	800
Gross profit	1,200
Fixed operating costs	600
Net operating income	$ 600

7. XYZ Corporation, another competitor of ABC Corporation, has fixed operating costs of $300 a year and variable costs of $6 a unit. XYZ also sells its product for $10 a unit. At a sales level of 200 units a year, total

2. operating leverage

5. $ 800
   1,200
   600

variable costs will be $_____, gross profit will be $_____, and net operating income will be $_____ . XYZ uses *more/less* operating leverage than ABC.

8. Refer again to Frames 3 and 7. If sales per company increase to 300 units a year, net operating income for ABC will be $_____, and net operating income for XYZ will be $_____ .

Skip to Frame 11 if you got the correct answer.

9. The answer to Frame 8 is as follows:

Company	ABC	XYZ
Sales ($10 x 300)	$3,000	$3,000
Variable costs	1,500	$1,800
Gross profit	1,500	1,200
Fixed operating costs	500	300
Net operating income	$1,000	$ 900

10. If sales for ABC expand to 500 units, net operating income will be $_____ .

11. Use the information from Frames 3, 7, and 8 to fill in the following table:

Company	ABC		XYZ	
Sales (units)	200	300	200	300
Sales (dollars)	(a)_____	(b)_____	(c)_____	(d)_____
Net operating income	(e)_____	(f)_____	(g)_____	(h)_____
Percent increase in sales		(i) _____		(j) _____
Percent increase in net operating income		(k)_____		(l) _____

---

7. $1,200
    800
    500
    less

8. $1,000
    900

10. $2,000

11. (a) $2,000   (b) $3,000   (c) $2,000   (d) $3,000
    (e)   500   (f)   1,000   (g)   500   (h)   900
                (i)   50%   (j)   50%
                (k)   100%   (l)   80%

12. For both companies, the percent increase in net operating income is greater than the percent increase in sales. Therefore, both companies are using some operating leverage. ABC Corporation showed a *greater/smaller* increase in net operating income than XYZ for the same percent increase in sales. Therefore, ABC is using *more / less* operating leverage than XYZ.

13. While we have said that ABC uses more operating leverage than XYZ, it is possible to be more precise. We can use a measurement known as the *degree of operating leverage*. The degree of operating leverage (D.O.L.) is computed as follows:

$$\text{D.O.L.} = \frac{\text{Percent increase in net operating income}}{\text{Percent increase in sales}}$$

14. The degree of operating leverage for ABC in the previous problem is:

$$\text{D.O.L.} = \frac{100\%}{50\%} = \underline{\hspace{2cm}}$$

15. From Frame 11, the degree of operating leverage for XYZ is \underline{\hspace{3cm}} .

Skip to Frame 18 if you got the correct answer.

16. The answer to Frame 15 is based on the material from Frame 11. Sales for XYZ increased from $2,000 to $3,000 or \underline{\hspace{2cm}}%. Net operating income increased from $500 to $900 or \underline{\hspace{2cm}}%. Using the formula in Frame 13, the degree of operating leverage is:

$$\text{D.O.L.} = \frac{80\%}{50\%} = \underline{\hspace{2cm}}$$

17. Refer again to Frame 5. Sales for Horizon were $\underline{\hspace{2cm}}$ and net operating income was $\underline{\hspace{2cm}}$. If the company had increased sales to 300 units, net operating income would have increased to $\underline{\hspace{2cm}}$. This represents a 50% increase in sales and a

---

12. greater
    more

14. 2

15. 1.6

16. 50%
    80%
    80/50 = 1.6

_____ % increase in net operating income. Therefore, the degree of operating leverage for Horizon Corporation is _____ .

18. The degree of operating leverage is a very handy measure. In addition to serving as an indication of which company has the highest operating leverage, it is a quick method for estimating the effect of a change in sales on net operating income. We can, with a little manipulation, restate the formula in Frame 13 as:

% change in net operating income = % change in sales x D.O.L.

19. For ABC Corporation with a D.O.L. of 2, a 10% increase in sales would bring about a 10% x 2 = _____% increase in net operating income.
This answer can be verified as follows:

	prior	+10%
Sales	$2,000	$2,200
Variable costs	1,000	1,100
Gross profit	1,000	1,100
Fixed operating costs	500	500
Net operating income	$ 500	$ 600

Percent increase in net operating income _____

20. For XYZ with a D.O.L. of 1.6, a 10% increase in sales would bring about a _____% increase in net operating income.

Skip to Frame 23 if you got the correct answer.

21. The answer to Frame 20 was found using the formula from Frame 18.

% change in net operating income = % change in sales x D.O.L.
% change in net operating income = 10% x 1.6 = 16%

---

17. $2,000
       600
     1,200
  · 102%
        2

19. 20%
    20%

20. 16%

22. For XYZ, a 20% increase in sales would result in a _____ % increase in net operating income.

23. Since the degree of operating leverage is frequently useful, it is fortunate that there is a fast, simple formula:

$$\text{D.O.L.} = \frac{\text{sales - variable costs}}{\text{sales - variable costs - fixed operating costs}}$$

24. If we use this formula to evaluate ABC corporation (Frame 3) at a sales level of $2,000, the degree of operating leverage is:

$$\text{D.O.L.} = \frac{\$2,000 - \$1,000}{\$2,000 - \$1,000 - \$500} = \text{_____}$$

25. For XYZ Corporation (Frame 7), the degree of operating leverage is computed as _____ using the formula in Frame 23.

Skip to Frame 28 if you got the correct answer.

26. The answer to Frame 25 is computed as follows:

$$\text{D.O.L.} = \frac{\$2,000 - \$1,200}{\$2,000 - \$1,200 - \$300} = 1.6$$

27. New Corporation has sales of $1,000, variable costs of $500, and fixed costs of $300. The D.O.L. for New Corporation is _____ . Using the formula in Frame 18, a 10% increase in sales would result in a _____ % increase in net operating income for New Corporation. In other words, if sales for New Corporation increased 10% to $1,200, net operating income would increase by 25% from the present level of $200 to $_____ .

28. It should be pointed out that the degree of operating leverage for a company is not the same at every level of sales. This is because the effect of operating leverage declines as sales reach higher levels and fixed costs become a smaller portion of total costs.

---

22. 32%

24. 2

25. 1.6

27. 2.5
    25%
    $250

29. For ABC Corporation (Frame 24) we computed the D.O.L. as _____ at a sales level of 200 units or $2,000. If we re-evaluate the degree of operating leverage at 300 units of sales, we get:

$$\text{D.O.L.} = \frac{\$3,000 - \$1,500}{\$3,000 - \$1,500 - \$500} = \underline{\hspace{2cm}}$$

We notice that the degree of operating leverage is *greater/less* at 300 units of sales than it was at 200 units of sales.

30. For XYZ Corporation (Frames 7 and 25) the degree of operating leverage at a sales level of 200 units was _____ . If we re-evaluate XYZ at 300 units of sales, the degree of operating leverage is _____ .

Skip to Frame 34 if you got the correct answer.

31. The answer to Frame 30 is based on the original problem stated in Frame 7. At a sales level of 300 units or $3,000, variable costs are $6 x 300 = $1,800 and fixed operating costs are $300. Using the formula in Frame 23, the degree of operating leverage is:

$$\text{D.O.L.} = \frac{\$3,000 - \$1,800}{\$3,000 - \$1,800 - \$300} = 1.33$$

32. New Corporation sells its product for $10 per unit, has variable costs of $5 per unit, and has fixed operating costs of $300 per year. At a sales level of 100 units or $1,000, total variable costs would be $5 x 100 = $_____ , and the degree of operating leverage would be:

$$\text{D.O. L.} = \frac{\$1,000 - \$500}{\$1,000 - \$500 - \$300} = \frac{\$500}{\$200} = \underline{\hspace{2cm}} .$$

33. At a sales level of 300 units or $3,000 total variable costs for New Corporation would be $_____ , and the degree of operating leverage would be _____ .

---

29. 2
   1.5
   less

30. 1.6
   1.33

32. $500
   2.5

33. $1,500
   1.25

If you had difficulty with Frame 33, go back to Frame 23 and work forward again before continuing.

34. The degree of operating leverage is a measure of both the potential return to the firm and the risk faced by the firm. Another look at ABC and XYZ Corporations will confirm this. From the previous analysis we concluded that when evaluated at a sales level of 200 units, ABC's degree of operating leverage was 2 and XYZ's degree of operating leverage was 1.6. At 200 units of sales, net operating income for both corporations was $500. If sales for both corporations increased by 50% to 300 units, ABC's net operating income would increase by 50% x 2 = _____ % to $_____, and XYZ's net operating income would increase by 50% x 1.6 = _____ % to $_____. ABC's net operating income clearly increased more because the company is using *more/less* operating leverage. On the other hand, if sales had declined 50%, net operating income for ABC would have declined 100% to $_____, and net operating income for XYZ would have declined 80% to $_____. While higher operating leverage allowed ABC to gain more from increased sales, it also caused net operating income for ABC to decline more during a period of declining sales.

35. We would conclude that high operating leverage can provide greater returns at high levels of sales but creates *more / less* risk since it results in smaller returns at low levels of sales.

B. FINANCIAL LEVERAGE

36. Financial leverage is defined as the use of funds for which a fixed return is paid. An example of the use of financial leverage is the financing of a portion of assets with debt. The company pays a fixed return on debt and

---

34. 100%
    $1,000
    80%
    $900
    more
    $0
    $100

35. more

if it can earn a higher return on assets than the interest it pays on debt, return on the equity investment will be improved. Financial leverage also increases risk since interest must be paid by the company even if returns for the year are very low.

37. While all companies use some operating leverage, it would be quite possible to have a company with no financial leverage. A company financed entirely through *debt/equity* would have no financial leverage.

38. Amtec Corporation uses no financial leverage. All of Amtec's assets are financed by common stock. Amtec has total assets of $1,000. If Amtec experiences earning power (net operating income/total assets) of 24%, net operating income will be $1,000 x .24 = $_____. Amtec is subject to a 50% tax rate. Profit after tax for Amtec will be $240 - (.5 x 240) = $_____. Since Amtec financed all assets through common stock, total common stock investment must equal total assets of $_____ . Return on equity is therefore 120/1000 = _____%.

39. Hiflo Corporation also has total assets of $1,000 and earning power of 24%. Net operating income for Hiflo is also $_____. Hiflo financed 1/2 of its assets through debt and 1/2 through common stock. Hiflo pays 8% interest on debt. Total interest paid by Hiflo is .08 x $500 = $_____ , and earnings before tax are $240 - 40 = $_____ . Taxes are .50 x $200 = $_____, and earnings after tax are $200 - $100 = $_____. Since Hiflo has only $500 in equity investment, return on equity is 100/500 = _____%. Hiflo is therefore able to earn a higher return on equity than Amtec through the use of _____ _____.

37. equity

38. $240
120
1,000
12%

39. $240
40
200
100
100
20%
financial leverage

40. Midway Corporation has the same total assets, earning power, tax rate, and interest rate as Hiflo. Midway, however, finances 1/4 of its assets with debt and the remaining 3/4 with equity. Return on equity for Midway is _____%.

Skip to Frame 43 if you got the correct answer.

41. The answer to Frame 40 is computed as follows:

Net operating assets	$1,000
Earning power	.24
Net operating income	240
Interest (.08 x $250)	20
Earnings before tax	220
Tax	110
Earnings after tax	$ 110

Return on equity = 110/750 = 14.67%

42. New Corporation has the same total assets, tax rate, earning power, and interest rate as Hiflo. New Corporation, however, finances 3/4 of its assets with debt and the remaining 1/4 with equity. Return on equity for New Corporation is _____%.

43. Financial leverage is therefore quite helpful to the owners if the earning power is greater than the cost of the fixed return funds used. Amtec earned a return on equity of _____%, but Hiflo used financial leverage to achieve _____% return on equity.

44. Just as operating leverage results in greater percent fluctuations in net operating income than in sales, financial leverage results in greater percent fluctuations in earnings before tax and net income than in net operating income.

---

40. 14.67%

42. 90/250 = *36%*

43. 12%
       20%

45. If net operating income for Amtec (Frame 38) increased 25% to $300, earnings before tax would increase _____% to $_____.

Skip to Frame 48 if you got the correct answer.

46. The answer to Frame 45 is computed as follows:

			% increase
Net operating income	$240	$300	25%
Interest	0	0	
Earnings before tax	$240	$300	25%

47. If net operating income for Amtec increases 50% from $240 to $360, earnings before tax will increase _____% to $_____.

48. If net operating income for Hiflo (Frame 39) increases 25% from $240 to $300, earnings before tax will increase _____% to $_____.

Skip to Frame 51 if you got the correct answer.

49. The answer to Frame 48 is as follows:

			% increase
Net operating income	$240	$300	25%
Interest	40	40	
Earnings before tax	$200	$260	30%

50. If net operating income for Hiflo (Frame 39) increases 50% from $240 to $360, earnings before tax will increase _____% to $_____.

51. Note that for Amtec (Frame 45) with no financial leverage, the percent increase in earnings before tax was *greater than/the same as/less than* net

---

45. 25%
$300

47. 50%
$360

48. 30%
$260

50. 60%
$320

operating income. For Hiflo with financial leverage, the percent increase in earnings before tax was *greater than/the same as/less than* the percent increase in net operating income. Thus, financial leverage causes earnings before tax to fluctuate proportionately *more/less* than operating income.

52. Just as you were able to compute a degree of operating leverage defined as percent change in net operating income ÷ percent change in sales, you can compute a degree of financial leverage defined as:

$$\text{D.F.L.} = \frac{\text{percent change in earnings before tax}}{\text{percent change in net operating income}}$$

53. At a net operating income of $240, the degree of financial leverage for Amtec (Frames 45 and 46) is 25%/25% = _____. At net operating income of $240, the degree of financial leverage for Hiflo (Frame 48) is:

D.F.L. = _____ ÷ _____ = _____ .

54. For Hiflo, at a net operating income of $200, earnings before tax would be $_____. As noted previously, earnings before tax would be $200 if net operating income were $240. Therefore, at a net operating income of $200, a _____% increase in net operating income would bring about a _____% increase in earnings before taxes.

D.F.L. = _____ ÷ _____ = _____

Skip to Frame 57 if you got the correct answer.

55. The answer to Frame 54 is as follows:

			% increase
Net operating income	$200	$240	20%
Interest	40	40	
Earnings before tax	$160	$200	25%

---

51. the same as
    greater than
    more

53. 1.0
    .30 ÷ .25 = 1.2

54. $160
    20%
    25%
    25%/20% = 1.25

D.F.L. = .25/.20 = 1.25

56. At a net operating income of $80, earnings before tax for Hiflo would be $_____, and at net operating income of $100 earnings before tax would be $_____. Therefore, a _____% increase in net operating income would bring about a _____% increase in earnings before tax. The degree of financial leverage at a net operating income of $80 is therefore:

D.F.L. = _____ ÷ _____ = _____ .

57. Fortunately, there is an easy formula to use in computing the degree of financial leverage. The formula for computing the degree of financial leverage is:

$$\text{D.F.L.} = \frac{\text{net operating income}}{\text{net operating income - interest}}$$

58. Use this formula to solve for Hiflo's degree of financial leverage at a net operating income of $240 (recall that interest was $40).

Skip to Frame 60 if you got the correct answer.

59. At a net operating income of $100, the degree of financial leverage for Hiflo would be _____ .

60. For Amtec (with no interest), the degree of financial leverage at net operating income of $200 (or any other level for that matter) would be

_____ .

61. The degree of financial leverage can be used to evaluate the effect of various changes in net operating income. For Hiflo, at a net operating income of $240, a 10% increase in net operating income would bring about an increase in earnings before tax of:

---

56. $40
   $60
   25%
   50%
   50%/25% = 2.0

58. 240/(240-40) = 1.2

59. 100/(100-40) = 1.67

60. 200/(200-0) = 1.0

% increase in earnings before tax = (% increase in N.O.I.) x (D.F.L.)

% increase in earnings before tax = .10 x 1.2 = _____

62. For Hiflo, a 50% increase in net operating income from $240 would result in a _____% increase in earnings before tax. In Frame 39, earnings before tax of $200 were computed at a net operating income level of $240. This 60% increase would raise earnings before tax to $_____ .

C. TOTAL LEVERAGE

63. You will recall that *financial / operating* leverage causes net operating income to fluctuate relatively more than sales, and *financial / operating* leverage causes earnings before tax to fluctuate relatively more than net operating income.

64. The financial results for Hiflo at sales levels of $600 and $660 appear below:

			Percent increased
Sales	$600	$660	10%
Variable costs	200	220	
Gross profit	400	440	
Fixed operating costs	200	200	
Net operating income	200	240	20%
Interest	40	40	
Earnings before tax	160	200	25%

For Hiflo, at a sales level of $600, the degree of operating leverage is _____, and the degree of financial leverage is _____ .

---

61. 12%

62. 50% x 1.2 = 60%
    $200 + .60 x $200 = *$320*

63. operating
    financial

64. 2.0
    1.25

65. Just as it is possible to compute a degree of financial leverage and a degree of operating leverage, it is also possible to compute a degree of total leverage. The formula for the *degree of total leverage* is:

$$\text{D.T.L.} = \frac{\text{percent increase in earnings before tax}}{\text{percent increase in sales}}$$

66. For Hiflo (Frame 64) the degree of total leverage is $.25/.10 =$ _____ .

67. The degree of total leverage can be computed by two other methods. These are illustrated below for Hiflo:

D.T.L. = D.O.L. x D.F.L.

D.T.L. = 2.0 x 1.25 = ————————

$$\text{D.T.L.} = \frac{\text{Sales - Variable Costs}}{\text{Sales - Variable Costs} - \text{Fixed Operating Costs - Interest}}$$

$$\text{D.T.L.} = \frac{600 - 200}{600 - 200 - 200 - 40} = \text{————————}$$

68. Like the degree of operating leverage and the degree of financial leverage, the degree of total leverage is not the same at all levels of sales. Compute the leverage for Hiflo at a sales level of $450 using the formulae in Frame 67.

D.O.L. = _____

D.F.L. = _____

D.T.L. = _____

Skip to Frame 71 if you got the correct answers.

———————————————————————————————————————

66. 2.5

67. 2.5
   2.5

68. 3.0
   1.67
   5.0

69. The answer to Frame 68 is computed as follows:

Sales	$450
Variable costs	150
Gross profit	300
Fixed operating costs	200
Net operating income	100
Interest	40
Earnings before tax	$ 60

$$\text{D.O.L.} = \frac{450 - 150}{450 - 150 - 200} = 3.0$$

$$\text{D.F.L.} = \frac{100}{100 - 40} = 1.67$$

$$\text{D.T.L.} = 1.67 \times 3.0 = 5.0$$

$$\text{D.T.L.} = \frac{450 - 150}{450 - 150 - 200 - 40} = 5.0$$

70. Compute the degree of operating leverage, degree of financial leverage, and the degree of total leverage for Hiflo at a sales level of $540:

D.O.L. = _____

D.F.L. = _____

D.T.L. = _____

71. Financial and operating leverage combine to give total leverage which causes profits to increase proportionately more than sales if sales increase, and *increase/decrease* proportionately more than sales if sales decrease.

D. BREAK-EVEN POINT

72. As discussed previously, higher financial and operating leverage leads to higher risk. One reason is because higher leverage leads to a higher

---

70. 2 1/4

    1 1/3

    3

71. decrease

break-even point. The break-even point is defined as the sales level necessary to just cover costs and leave the company with zero profit.

73. The break-even point in dollars of sales can be calculated using the following fomula:

$$\text{B.E.P.} = \frac{F + I}{1 - V/S}$$

where:

F = Fixed operating costs
I = Interest expense
S = Sales in dollars
V = Total variable costs

74. For Hiflo, using the information from Frame 64, the break-even point is $_____ of sales.

Skip to Frame 77 if you got the correct answer.

75. The answer to Frame 74 is computed as follows:

$$\text{B.E.P.} = \frac{200 + 40}{1 - 200/600} = \$360$$

76. Midway Corporation has fixed operating costs of $100 a year and interest expense of $100 a year. Sales this year were $500, and variable costs were $250. The break-even point for Midway is _____ .

77. If Hiflo had no interest payments, the break-even point would be

_____ .

78. The use of operating and financial leverage raises the break-even point and thereby *increases/decreases* risk.

---

74. $360

76. $(100 + 100)/(1 - 250/500) = 200/.5 = \$400$

77. $300

78. increases

79. The analysis of Hiflo can be summarized on a break-even chart. Recall that fixed operating costs were $200 and interest was $40, giving total fixed costs of $240. Variable costs were $200 at a sales level of $600, or 1/3 of sales. The line marked TR on the graph shows the total revenue which is, of course, equal to sales. At zero sales, total cost would be $240. At $600 of sales, total cost equals $240 + (600/3) = $440. By drawing a line passing through $240 at zero sales and $440 at $600 sales, the total cost line is completed. The Total revenue line crosses the total cost line at $_____ of sales. This is the break-even point computed in Frame 74.

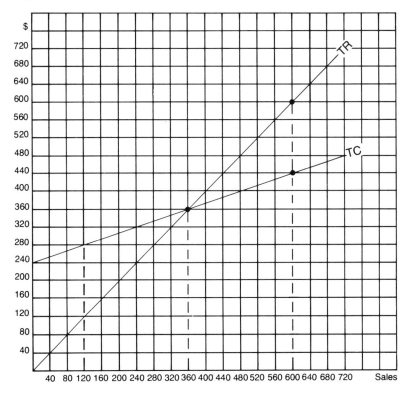

80. Above the break-even point, the difference between total revenue and total cost represents earnings before tax. Below the break-even point, the difference between the two lines represents a loss. The chart shows that at a sales level of $600, total cost for Hiflo is $ _____ , and earnings before tax are 600 − 440 = $ _____ . At a sales level of $480, total

---

79. $360

revenue is $_____, total cost is $_____, and earnings before
tax are $_____ . At a sales level of $120, total cost is $_____,
and the company suffers a loss of $_____ .

81. Southern Manufacturing Corporation had sales of $300 and variable costs
of $150. Fixed operating costs were $50 and interest was $50. Construct a
break-even chart for Southern.

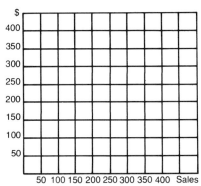

The correct break-even chart appears in Frame 82.

82. The break-even chart for Southern Manufacturing should appear as
follows:

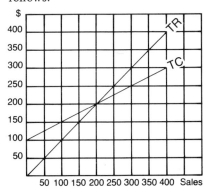

---

80. $440
   $160
   $480
   $400
   $ 80
   $280
   $160

83. Using the break-even chart for Southern find the break-even point _____, the earnings before tax at a sales level of $400 _____, and the loss at a sales level of $100 _____.

84. Once again, the break-even point gives an indication of risk exposure. A higher break-even point indicates *more* / *less* risk. The company may willingly accept a higher break-even point with the hope of increasing profitability.

SUMMARY

A. OPERATING LEVERAGE

1. Operating leverage is the use of fixed costs. If the company voluntarily chooses to increase fixed costs, it does so with the hope of reducing total costs. This, of course, also increases risk.

2. The *degree of operating leverage* is a measure of the effect of operating leverage on operating income. It is defined as follows:

$$D.O.L. = \frac{\text{percent increase in net operating income}}{\text{percent increase in sales}}$$

3. A convenient formula for determining the degree of operating leverage is:

$$D.O.L. = \frac{\text{sales - variable costs}}{\text{sales - variable costs - fixed operating costs}}$$

4. Factors affecting the degree of operating leverage:
   a. The greater the fixed operating costs, the greater will be the degree of operating leverage, other things being equal.
   b. As the level of sales increases, the degree of operating leverage decreases.

---

83. $200
    $100
    $50.

84. more

B. FINANCIAL LEVERAGE

1. Financial leverage is defined as the use of funds for which a fixed return is paid. Debt is an example of a fixed-return source of funds. The company uses financial leverage with the hope of increasing the return to owners.

2. The *degree of financial leverage* is a measure of the effect of financial leverage on profits. It is defined as follows:

$$\text{D.F.L.} = \frac{\text{percent increase in earnings before tax}}{\text{percent increase in net operating income}}$$

3. A convenient formula for computing the degree of financial leverage is:

$$\text{D.F.L.} = \frac{\text{net operating income}}{\text{net operating income} - \text{interest}}$$

4. Factors affecting the degree of financial leverage:
   a. An increase in interest will increase the degree of financial leverage, other things being equal.
   b. As the level of net operating income increases, the degree of financial leverage decreases, other things being equal.

C. DEGREE OF TOTAL LEVERAGE

1. The degree of total leverage is a measure of the combined effects of financial and operating leverage. It is defined as:

$$\text{D.T.L.} = \frac{\text{percent increase in earnings before tax}}{\text{percent increase in sales}}$$

2. The degree of total leverage can be computed by either of the following methods:

$$\text{D.T.L.} = \frac{\text{sales} - \text{variable costs}}{\text{sales} - \text{variable costs} - \text{fixed operating costs} - \text{interest}}$$

$$\text{D.T.L.} = \text{degree of operating leverage} \times \text{degree of financial leverage}$$

3. Factors affecting the degree of total leverage:
   a. Other things being equal, an increase in interest or fixed operating costs will increase the degree of total leverage.
   b. As the level of sales increases, the degree of total leverage decreases, other things being equal.

D. BREAK-EVEN POINT

1. The break-even point is the sales level necessary to just cover costs and leave the company with zero profit.

2. The break-even point can be computed using the following formula:

$$\text{B.E.P.} = \frac{\text{fixed operating costs} + \text{interest}}{1 - \text{variable costs/sales}}$$

3. Factors affecting the break-even point:
   a. The use of operating leverage will increase the break-even point.
   b. The use of financial leverage will increase the break-even point.

PROBLEMS

PROBLEM 1:

U.S. Products Corporation had sales of $100,000 last year. Variable costs were $50,000, and fixed operating costs were $25,000. Interest expense was $5,000.

a. Compute the degree of operating leverage.
b. Compute the degree of financial leverage.
c. Compute the degree of total leverage.
d. Compute the break-even point.
e. Compute the earnings before tax at a sales level of $100,000.
f. If sales increased 20% to $120,000, earnings before tax would increase _____ % to $_____ .
g. If sales decreased 20% to $80,000, earnings before tax would decrease _____ % to $_____ .
h. Prepare a break-even chart for U.S. Products.
i. From the break-even chart, find the earnings before tax at a sales level of $150,000 and a sales level of $20,000.

PROBLEM 2:

FCM Corporation manufactures the same product as U.S. but uses different production and financing methods. FCM also had sales of $100,000. Variable costs were $20,000, fixed operating costs were $40,000, and interest was $20,000.

a. Compute the degree of operating leverage.
b. Compute the degree of financial leverage.
c. Compute the degree of total leverage.

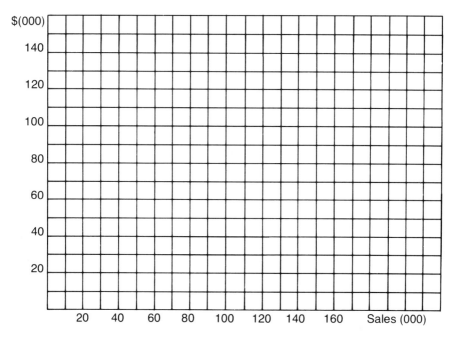

d. Compute the break-even point.
e. Compute the earnings before tax at a sales level of $100,000.
f. If sales increased 20% to $120,000, earnings before tax would increase
   _____ % to $_____ .
g. If sales decreased 20% to $80,000, earnings before tax would decrease
   _____ % to $_____ .
h. From the starting point of $100,000, if sales for each company increased by an equal amount, earnings before tax for which company would increase more?
i. From the starting point of $100,000, if sales for each company decreased by an equal amount, earnings before tax for which company would decrease more?

SOLUTIONS

SOLUTION 1:

U.S. Products Corporation

a. $\dfrac{\$100,000 - 50,000}{100,000 - 50,000 - 25,000} = 2.0$

b. $\dfrac{25,000}{25,000 - 5,000} = 1.25$

c. $\dfrac{100,000 - 50,000}{100,000 - 50,000 - 25,000 - 5,000} = 2.5$

d. $\dfrac{25,000 + 5,000}{1 - (50,000/100,000)} = \$60,000$

e.

Sales	$100,000
Variable costs	50,000
Gross profit	50,000
Fixed cost	25,000
Net operating income	25,000
Interest	5,000
Earnings before tax	20,000

f. 20% x 2.5 = *50%*

   1.50 x $20,000 = *$30,000*

g. -20% x 2.5 = *-50%*

   .50 x $20,000 = *$10,000*

h. The total cost line should cross the vertical axis at $30,000. The total revenue line should cross the vertical axis at $0. The two lines should intersect at $60,000 of sales.

i. $45,000; -$20,000

SOLUTION 2:

FCM Corporation

a. $\dfrac{100,000 - 20,000}{100,000 - 20,000 - 40,000} = 2$

b. $\dfrac{40,000}{40,000 - 20,000} = 2$

c. $\dfrac{100,000 - 20,000}{100,000 - 20,000 - 40,000 - 20,000} = 4$

d. $\dfrac{40,000 + 20,000}{1 - (20,000/100,000)} = \$75,000$

e.

Sales	$100,000
Variable costs	20,000
Gross profit	80,000
Fixed cost	40,000
Net operating income	40,000
Interest	20,000
Earnings before tax	20,000

 f. 20% x 4 = *80%*

  1.80 x $20,000 = *$36,000*

 g. -20% x 4 = *80%*

  .20 x $20,000 = *$4,000*

 h. FCM Corporation

 i. FCM Corporation

4
WORKING CAPITAL MANAGEMENT

Working capital management refers to the management of current assets and current liabilities. This is of particular importance in that current assets represent over half of the assets of the typical business firm, and current liabilities represent a major claim against liquidity. Since they do represent a major portion of the assets of the firm, the management of current assets can greatly affect profitability. Great care is required in directing investment so that only the current assets which can be justified by a sufficient contribution to profits are chosen. Similarly, care is required in establishing a current liability structure so as to be reasonably confident that the claims can be met as they fall due.

The term *working capital* refers to the total current assets of the firm. The primary current assets are cash, accounts receivable, and inventory. Profitability is the primary guideline in current asset management. Current assets are not "productive" in the same sense that a manufacturing plant is productive. They do, however, contribute to profitability in that they are necessary to the successful operation of the business. Careful management is necessary to assure that the optimum current asset level in terms of profitability is maintained. The cash balance itself earns no return, but it decreases risk of insolvency and avoids the costs connected with missed payments and frequent short term borrowing of small amounts.

In the case of inventory, there are three main costs, the sum of which the manager wishes to minimize. These costs are inventory carrying costs, including the cost of funds tied up, ordering costs, and the opportunity cost of lost sales due to lack of inventory. The two major decisions that are made in an effort to minimize these costs are the inventory level at which a new order is placed and the amount of inventory that is ordered each time.

For accounts receivable, the major costs are the cost of funds tied up, and the bad debt loss. Accounts receivable policy, of course, directly affects sales and therefore profits. The major accounts receivable decisions are to whom to grant credit, what the time is between the sale and the due date for payment, what degree of discounts for prompt payment, and the level of collection effort on past due accounts. The careful balancing of these costs and benefits will have a major effect on the profitability of the firm.

The major current liabilities are accounts payable, accrued liabilities, and short term loans. Many of the current liabilities are cost free in the sense that no direct interest payment is made, and the interest rate on short term debt is usually lower than that for long term debt. However, current liabilities present a claim against liquidity that could lead to financial difficulty in times of stress. The goal of current liability management is to select a mix of current liabilities and a total level of current liabilities which achieve satisfactory trade-off between the cost and risk.

Upon completion of this chapter you will understand the fundamental principles and techniques of working capital management. You will be able to determine the appropriate order quantity for inventory and understand the effect of the reorder point on total costs. You will be able to understand the effect of accounts receivable policy on profitability and the interest effect of credit terms. You will also be able to prepare a cash budget to plan for future cash needs and levels of cash. In addition, you will be able to evaluate the cost of various sources of short term debt and to estimate the appropriate level of total current liabilities.

A. INTRODUCTION TO WORKING CAPITAL

1. The term _____ is identical with the term current assets. The term _____ _____ _____refers to current assets minus current liabilities, or the amount by which short term uses of funds exceed short term sources.

2. Working capital is of interest because it affects both the risk position of the firm and the return on assets. Atel Corporation has total assets of

Skip to Frame 4 if you got the correct answer.

---

1. working capital
   net working capital

$1,000, consisting of working capital of $500 and fixed assets of $500. Atel has net operating income of $200 and earning power of _____%.

3. Earning power of Atel is:

$$\frac{\text{Net Operating Income}}{\text{Total Assets}} = \frac{\$\,200}{\$1000} = 20\%$$

Refer to Frame 49 of Chapter 1 for a review of earning power.

4. If Atel were able to reduce working capital to $300 without decreasing net operating income, total assets would be decreased to $_____ and earning power would be increased to _____%.

5. Working capital levels also affect profitability in that decreased accounts receivable and inventory levels are normally achieved at the expense of decreased sales. Decreased working capital is also achieved at the expense of decreased liquidity reserves and, therefore, increased risk of liquidity problems. Working capital policy is aimed at the optimal trade-off between these various factors.

B. INVENTORY MANAGEMENT

6. As shown in Frame 3, the level of investment in inventory affects total assets and therefore earning power. It also affects sales since decreased inventory levels increase the probability of stock-outs and lost sales. The object of inventory management is to minimize total inventory costs. Total inventory costs consist of:

T.I.C.=Ordering Costs + Carrying Costs + Lost Sales Opportunity Cost

The two major inventory decisions are the reorder point, or the inventory level at which a new order is placed, and the reorder quantity, or the quantity that is ordered each time.

7. As the reorder quantity increases carrying costs increase and ordering costs decrease. The goal is to select a reorder quantity that minimizes the sum of

---

2. 20%

4. $800
   200/800 = 25%

these costs. The reorder quantity which achieves this minimum cost is found by the following formula:

ROQ = $\sqrt{(2xSx0)/C}$

where:

S = Total demand for the period in units

0 = Ordering costs per order

C = Carrying cost per unit per period

8. ABC Corporation sells 50,000 units of their product per year. Ordering costs are $100 per order, and carrying costs are $10 per unit per year. The optimal reorder quantity is:

ROQ = $\sqrt{(2 \times 50,000 \times 100)/10}$ = $\sqrt{1,000,000}$ = _____

9. American Corporation has sales of 25,000 units per year for a particular product. Ordering costs are $50 per order and carrying costs are $10 per year. The optimal order quantity is _____ units.

Skip to Frame 11 if you got the correct answer.

10. Southeast Corporation sells 100,000 units per year of a particular product. Order costs are $80 per order and carrying costs are $4 per unit per year. The optimal order quantity is _____ units.

11. The reorder point, or the inventory level at which a new order is placed, affects both the lost sales opportunity cost and the inventory carrying cost. As the reorder point increases, the probability of lost sales due to lack of inventory decreases. Unfortunately, a high reorder point leads to higher average inventory and therefore higher inventory carrying costs. The objective in establishing a reorder point policy is to make the optimum trade-off between inventory carrying cost and the lost sales opportunity cost. The choice of a reorder point policy that will minimize these costs is illustrated in the following frames.

---

8. 1,000 units

9. $\sqrt{(2 \times 25,000 \times 50)/10}$ = $\sqrt{250,000}$ = *500*

10. $\sqrt{(2 \times 100,000 \times 80)/4}$ = $\sqrt{4,000,000}$ = *2,000*

12. Southern Technical Corporation is considering their reorder point policy. If demand exceeds supply, they lose sales. The opportunity cost is $1 per unit of lost sales. It takes one month for new inventory to arrive. At a reorder point of 100 units, the inventory carrying cost is $50 per month. They have observed that orders for 100 units are received during 50% of the months, and for 200 units during the remaining 50%. The optimum reorder quantity has been determined to be 150 units, so they expect to place an order about once a month. Reorder costs are expected to average $20 per month regardless of the reorder point. If the company uses a 100 unit reorder point, total inventory cost will be as shown below:

Reorder Point	Orders	Lost Orders	Lost Order Opportunity Cost	Probability	Expected Opportunity Cost
100	100	0	0	0.5	0
	200	100	$100	0.5	$50
			Total Expected Opportunity Cost =		$50

Expected Total Inventory   = Ordering + Carrying + Opportunity
Cost Per Month   Cost   Cost   Cost

            = $20   + $50   + $50   =   _____

If the company experiences orders for 100 units in a month, it will lose no sales. If orders for the month are 200 units, there will be unfilled demand for 100 units at an opportunity cost of $1 per unit, or $100. Since they expect orders for 200 units during 50% of the months, the average, or expected lost order opportunity cost is .5 x 100 = $50.

13. If Southern uses a 200 unit reorder point, inventory carrying cost will be $125 per month, but lost order opportunity cost will decline. Compute the total inventory cost per month using a 200 unit reorder point.

Reorder Point	Orders	Lost Orders	Lost Order Opportunity Cost	Probability	Expected Opportunity Cost
200	100	_____	_____	0.5	_____
	200	_____	_____	0.5	_____
			Total Expected Opportunity Cost =		_____

Expected Total Inventory   = Ordering + Carrying + Opportunity
Cost Per Month   Cost   Cost   Cost

            = _____   +   _____   +   _____   =   _____

_____

12. $120   13. Expected total inventory cost per month = $145.

Skip to Frame 16 if you got the correct answer.

14. At a 200 unit reorder point, lost orders will be zero even if demand reaches 200 units. Therefore, demand is never expected to exceed supply, and the lost order opportunity cost is expected to be $_____. The inventory carrying cost is given as $125 per month, and the order cost will average $20 per month. Total expected inventory cost per month is therefore $20 + $125 + $0 = _____.

15. At a reorder point of 150 units, the inventory carrying cost for Southern would be $90 per month. Compute the expected total inventory cost for Southern based on a 150 unit reorder point.

Reorder Point	Orders	Lost Orders	Lost Orders Opportunity Cost	Probability	Expected Opportunity Cost
150	100	_____	_____	0.5	_____
	200	_____	_____	0.5	_____

Total Expected Opportunity Cost = _____

$$\text{Expected Total Inventory Cost Per Month} = \frac{\text{Ordering} + \text{Carrying} + \text{Opportunity}}{\text{Cost} \quad \text{Cost} \quad \text{Cost}}$$

= _____ + _____ + _____ = _____

16. Of the reorder points evaluated for Southern the one giving the lowest total inventory cost per month is _____ units. At a reorder point of 100 units, total inventory cost per month is $_____.

---

14. $0
    $145

15.

Reorder Point	Orders	Lost Orders	Lost Order Opportunity Cost	Probability	Expected Opportunity Cost
150	100	0	0	0.5	0
	200	50	$50	0.5	$25
					$25

16. 100 $120

Expected T.I.C. Per Month = *$20 + $90 + $25 = $135.*

17. If the opportunity cost per unit of lost sales were $2, the lowest total inventory cost would be achieved at a reorder point of *100 / 200* units. *Skip to Frame 20 if you got the correct answer.*

18. The cost analysis for Frame 17 appears below:

Reorder Point	Orders	Lost Orders	Lost Order Opportunity Cost	Probability	Expected Opportunity Cost
100	100	0	0	0.5	$ 0
	200	100	200	0.5	100
					$100
200	100	0	0	0.5	$ 0
	200	0	0	0.5	0
					$ 0

100: Expected T.I.C. per month = $20 + $50 + $100 = $170

200: Expected T.I.C. per month = $20 + $125 + $0 = $145

In this case, total cost is lower ($145) at a reorder point of 200 units.

19. At a lost order opportunity cost of $1.50 per unit, expected T.I.C. per month would be $_____ for a 100 unit reorder point and $_____ for a 200 unit reorder point.

20. The main two variables in inventory management are the _____ _____ and _____ _____. The objective of inventory management is to minimize total inventory cost which consists of:

T.I.C. = _____ + _____ + _____

---

17. 200

19. $20 + $50 + $75 = *$145*
$20 + $125 + $0 = *$145*

20. reorder point
reorder quantity
Ordering cost + Carrying cost + Opportunity cost

Since a lower opportunity cost and order cost are achieved at the expense of higher inventory carrying cost, the optimum inventory policy is the best trade-off between the various costs to achieve the lowest overall cost.

C. ACCOUNTS RECEIVABLE MANAGEMENT

21. Accounts receivable management affects profitability in several ways. First, funds tied up in accounts receivable would otherwise be available to invest elsewhere. Second, a more liberal credit policy increases the risk of bad debt loss. The offsetting factor is that accounts receivable policy can be used to increase sales and profits. The objective of accounts receivable management is to make the optimum trade-off between the expenses connected with accounts receivable policy and the sales generating effect of such policy. The major decisions in accounts receivable management are to whom to give credit (credit standards), and on what terms to sell (credit terms). A third policy area deals with the collection effort made on delinquent accounts. The financial effects of accounts receivable policy are of particular interest. Among the financial effects are the amount of funds tied up in accounts receivable, the amount of bad debt loss, and the additional sales attributable to accounts receivable policy.

22. The first area to be considered is credit terms. Credit terms include the number of days from the invoice date until payment is due and the discount for prompt payment, if any. Credit terms are stated in abbreviated form similar to the following:

2/10, net 30

These particular terms mean that the buyer is required to pay within 30 days of the invoice date but receives a 2% discount for early payment if he pays within 10 days.

23. Celestial Products sells on terms of 3/30 net 90. This means that payment is due _____ days from the invoice date but a _____ % discount is allowed if the account is paid within _____ days of the invoice date.

---

23. 90
    3%
    30

Skip to Frame 25 if you got the correct answer.

24. Terms of 2/20, net 60 indicate that payment is due _____ days after the invoice date but a _____% discount is allowed if the account is paid within _____ days of the invoice date.

25. The effect of the discount is normally to make it rather expensive to wait until the due date to pay the bill. For example, a customer who buys $100 worth of goods on terms of 2/10, net 30, pays only $98 if payment is made by the 10th day. To wait until the 30th day, the customer pays the full $100 or a 2/98 = 2.04% fee for the use of the money from the 10th to the 30th day. He pays the 2.04% for using the money for (30-10)/365 = 1/18.25 of a year. This is equivalent to an annual interest rate of:

$$\frac{2}{98} \times \frac{365}{30-10} \times .0204 \times 18.25 = \underline{\hspace{3cm}} \%$$

26. If a company buys on terms of 2/30, net 90 and pays on the 90th day, it is equivalent to paying an interest of _____% for the 60-day period or an annual interest rate of _____%.

Skip to Frame 28 if you got the correct answer.

27. Paying on the 45th day when buying on terms of 2/15, net 45 is equivalent to paying an annual interest rate of _____%.

28. From the point of view of the seller, the longer the credit terms, the more funds are tied up in accounts receivable. The question is whether the increased sales justify the increased funds tied up.

29. ABC Corporation is considering a change in credit terms from the present net 30 (no discount is given for early payment) to net 60. Sales per year

---

24. 60
    2%
    20

25. 37.2%

26. 2.04%   •
    2.04 x 365/ (90-30) = 2.04 x 6.08 = *12.4%*

27. 2/98 x 365/30 = .0204 x 12.17 = .248 = *24.8%*

are presently $1,460 and would be expected to increase to $1,752 if the new credit policy were adopted. The new level of sales could be met without increasing any asset except accounts receivable. The anticipated effects of the proposed change in credit policy are shown below:

Credit Terms	Net 30	Net 60	Change
Sales Per Year	$1,460	$1,752	$292
Net Operating Income	184	234	50
Accounts Receivable	120	288	168
Total Assets	1,000	1,168	168

Under the present credit policy earning power is $184/$1,000 = _____ %. A change to the proposed credit policy would produce a $_____ increase in net operating income and would require a $_____ increase in total assets. The return on this additional investment is 50/168 = _____%. ABC is willing to invest in any project with a rate of return above their present earning power. The new credit policy *does / does not* appear to be attractive from ABC's point of view.

30. By selling for cash only, ABC can reduce total assets to $880. However, it is estimated that they would also reduce sales to $1,000 and net operating income to $124. If the company wishes to invest in all opportunities providing returns greater than their present earning power, would cash terms be better than the present net 30 terms? _____ . Above what required rate of return would the company prefer the cash terms to net 30 terms? _____ .

Skip to Frame 33 if you got the correct answer.

31. To answer this question, you must ask what rate of return is earned on the marginal investment required to go from cash terms to net thirty terms and what incremental net operating income is involved. From cash terms to net thirty terms, net operating income increases $184 − $124 = *$60.*

---

29. 18.4%
    $50
    $168
    29.8%
    does

30. no
    50%

Total investment increases $1,000 − $880 = *$120*. The return on the marginal investment is $60/$120 = *$50*. Cash terms would *not* be preferred over net thirty terms unless the required rate of return exceeded *50%*.

32. If ABC could change to cash terms with a resultant profit decrease to only $164, the return on the marginal investment to go from cash to net 30 credit terms would be _____ ÷ _____ = _____ %. If 18.4% was the required rate of return, they should sell on terms of *cash / net 30*.

33. Credit terms are the first part of credit policy. The second part is the question of *credit standards*, or to whom to grant credit. By being more liberal in granting credit, the company can increase sales. At the same time, however, the more liberal terms increase bad debt losses. Once again the decision is made with the objective of maximizing profitability.

34. American Wholesale is considering a change in credit standards. The company currently has sales of $800,000 per year and net operating income of $20,000. Total assets are presently $100,000. By selling to a new group of customers, they could increase sales by $200,000 and net operating income by $10,000 before allowing for bad debt losses. However, they estimate that 2.5% of the new sales would be uncollectable. The increased net operating income from the new sales would be $10,000 − .025($200,000) = $5,000. The new sales would require an increase in total assets of $30,000. The return on this $30,000 marginal investment is therefore $5,000/$30,000 = _____ %. If the required return for American is the present earning power of 20%, the new customers *would/would not* be attractive.

35. If the above customers were expected to result in a bad debt loss of only 1.5%, the return on the marginal investment would be _____ % and the new group of customers *would / would not* be attractive.

Skip to Frame 38 if you got the correct answer.

---

32. 184 - 164 = 20
1000 - 880 = 120
20 ÷ 120 = 16.7%
cash

34. 16.7%
would not

35. 23.3%
would

36. The answer to Frame 35 is computed as follows: the increase in net operating income from the new sale would be $10,000 - .015($200,000) = *$7,000* and the return on the marginal investment of $30,000 would be $7,000/$30,000 = *23.33%*. This is above their required rate of return, and the new group of customers would be an attractive investment.

37. For Southeast Corporation, variable costs (excluding bad debt loss) are 80% of sales. A new group of customers would require an increase in total assets of $100,000 and would increase sales by approximately $200,000 per year. Bad debt losses equalling 5% of sales are expected for this group of customers. Southeast requires earning power of 20% on all investments. The marginal investment to acquire this group of customers would provide a return of _____%. These customers *would / would not* be attractive.

38. In summary, the goals of both accounts receivable and inventory management are the profitability of the firm. Both policies involve investments. These investments must provide a satisfactory rate of return to the company. The higher the reorder point and the higher the reorder quantity, the *greater / less* will be the investment in inventory. The increased investment is expected to result in increased net operating income. The question is whether the increased net operating income is sufficient to provide a high enough rate of return on the increased investment. More liberal credit standards and credit terms are expected to result in more sales and *more / less* net operating income. The question is whether the increase in net operating income is sufficient to provide a satisfactory return on the additional investment.

D. CASH BUDGETING

39. Cash on hand is also an investment in that it consists of funds that could otherwise by employed elsewhere. Increased cash levels result in foregone investment opportunities, but decreased cash levels increase the chance of

---

37. $200,000 - .8($200,000) - .05($200,000) = $30,000
    $30,000/$100,000 = *30%*
    would

38. greater
    more

liquidity problems. It is important to project cash flows as accurately as possible to minimize the required cash balance and also hold liquidity problems to a minimum. The tool for accomplishing this is the *cash budget*.

40. The cash budget is merely a summary of all projected cash flows for a period of time. The cash budget is usually prepared for a relatively limited time period, such as a year. It is normally broken down into sub-periods. A common approach would be to prepare a cash budget by month for the next year. The normal starting point for such a budget is to prepare a sales forecast by month. From the sales forecast it is possible to estimate collections of accounts receivable, payments for inventory, and other cash payments. The cash budget deals only with cash and does not consider non-cash expense items.

41. Powell Wholesale Supply has a January 1 cash balance of $15,000. The actual sales for December and the forecasted sales for the first four months of the year are shown below. The company is preparing a cash budget for the first three months of the year.

Month	December	January	February	March	April
Sales	$20,000	$30,000	$30,000	$40,000	$50,000

The company sells its goods on terms of net 30, and they have little difficulty with delinquent accounts. Therefore, all of December's sales are collected in January, all of January's sales are collected in February, etc.

Month	December	January	February	March	April
Sales	$20,000	$30,000	$30,000	$40,000	$50,000
Collection of Accounts Receivable		20,000	_____	_____	

Collection of accounts receivable is the company's only source of cash.

---

41. February = $30,000; March = $30,000

42. The next step is to identify the cash outflows. The company has a cost of goods sold equal to 50% of sales, and goods are purchased for cash one month in advance of sales. December inventory purchases, therefore, were .50 × $30,000 = *$15,000*. Fill in the inventory purchases for January through March below:

Month	December	January	February	March	April
Sales	$20,000	$30,000	$30,000	$40,000	$50,000
Purchase of Inventory	15,000	_____	_____	_____	

43. In addition to purchase of inventory, Powell has certain other expenses. The company pays wages of $10,000 per month, rent of $1,500 per month, and utilities of $500 per month. In addition, a lease payment of $2,000 is due in February. Complete the portion of the cash budget shown below.

Month	December	January	February	March	April
Sales	$20,000	$30,000	$30,000	$40,000	$50,000
Collection of Accounts Receivable		20,000	30,000	30,000	
Purchase of Inventory		15,000	20,000	25,000	
Wages		_____	_____	_____	
Rent		_____	_____	_____	
Utilities		_____	_____	_____	
Lease Payment		_____	_____	_____	
Total Payments		_____	_____	_____	

---

42. January = $15,000; February = $20,000; March = $25,000

43.
Wages	$10,000	$10,000	$10,000
Rent	1,500	1,500	1,500
Utilities	500	500	500
Lease Payment	_____	2,000	_____
Total Payments	$27,000	$34,000	$37,000

44. Having completed the collections of accounts receivable (the only form of cash inflow in this case) and the total payments, the next step is to find the net cash flow for each month. Complete the table below.

Month	December	January	February	March
Collection of Accounts Receivable		$20,000	$30,000	$30,000
Total Payments		27,000	34,000	37,000
Net Cash Flow		($ 7,000)		

45. The next step is to project the short-term borrowing needs and repayment schedules. The company had a cash balance of $15,000 on December 31 and must maintain a minimum cash balance of $8,000. Compute their borrowing needs below.

	December	January	February	March
Net Cash Flow		($ 7,000)	($ 4,000)	($ 7,000)
Beginning Cash		15,000		
Unadjusted Balance		8,000		
Borrow (Repay)				
Ending Cash Balance		$ 8,000		
Cumulative Short Term Borrowing		$ 0		

The correct answer appears in Frame 46.

46. You have now completed the three-month cash budget in steps. The results are brought together and summarized on page 92.

---

44. February = *($4,000)*; March = *($7,000)*

	December	January	February	March	April
Sales	$20,000	$30,000	$30,000	$40,000	$50,000
Collection of					
Accounts Receivable		20,000	30,000	30,000	
Purchase of Inventory		15,000	20,000	25,000	
Wages		10,000	10,000	10,000	
Rent		1,500	1,500	1,500	
Utilities		500	500	500	
Lease Payment		___	2,000	___	
Total Payments		$27,000	$34,000	$37,000	
Net Cash Flows		(7,000)	(4,000)	7,000	
Beginning Cash		15,000	8,000	8,000	
Unadjusted Balance		8,000	4,000	1,000	
Borrow (Repay)		___	4,000	(7,000)	
		$ 8,000	$ 8,000	$ 8,000	
Cumulative Borrowing		$ 0	$ 4,000	$11,000	

47. Powell's sales forecasts for May, June, and July are $40,000, $30,000, and $20,000, respectively. Wages, rent, and utilities will be the same as for the first three months of the year. Lease payments of $2,000 are due in April and June. They will repay portions of the $11,000 short term loan whenever they can do so without reducing the cash level below $8,000. Use the space below to prepare a cash budget for April through June.

	March	April	May	June	July
	$40,000	$50,000	$40,000	$30,000	$20,00
Sales					
Collection of					
Accounts Receivable					
Purchase of Inventory					
Wages					
Rent					
Utilities					
Lease Payments					
Total Payments					
Net Cash Flows					
Beginning Cash					
Unadjusted Cash Balance					
Borrow (Repay)					
Ending Cash Balance	$ 8,000				
Cumulative Borrowing	$11,000				

Skip to Frame 49 if you got the correct answer.

48. The answer to Frame 47 appears as follows:

	March	April	May	June	July
Sales	$40,000	$50,000	$40,000	$30,000	$20,000
Collection of					
Accounts Receivable [1]		40,000	50,000	40,000	
Purchases of Inventory [2]		20,000	15,000	10,000	
Wages [3]		10,000	10,000	10,000	
Rent [3]		1,500	1,500	1,500	
Utilities [3]		500	500	500	
Lease Payment [4]		2,000		2,000	
Total Payments		$34,000	$27,000	$24,000	
Net Cash Flows		6,000	23,000	16,000	
Beginning Cash		8,000	8,000	26,000	
Unadjusted Cash Balance		14,000	31,000	42,000	
Borrow (Repay)		(6,000)	(5,000)	0	
Ending Cash Balance	$ 8,000	$ 8,000	$26,000	$42,000	
Cumulative Borrowing	$11,000	5,000	0	0	

[1] Recall that they sell on terms of net 30, so April collections equal March sales, etc.

[2] Recall that inventory is purchased one month in advance of sales and the cost of inventory equals 50% of sales. Therefore, April inventory purchases are .50 x $40,000 = $20,000.

[3] Wages, rent, and utilities remain the same for each month.

[4] Lease payments of $2,000 in April and June are given.

Verify again the results shown and correct your original answer to Frame 47 before continuing.

49. Powell's August, September, and October sales are forecasted to be $20,000, $16,000, and $20,000, respectively. A $2,000 lease payment is due in August. Credit terms, wages, rent, and utilities remain the same as in previous months. Prepare a cash budget for July through September.

Solution space is provided on the following page.

---

47. Ending Cash Balance $8,000 $26,000 $42,000
        Cumulative Borrowing   5,000   0   0

Sales	June	July	August	September	October
	$30,000	$20,000	$20,000	$16,000	$20,000
	$42,000				
	0				

Locate and correct any errors in your answer before continuing.

50. The cash balances and borrowing needs of Powell Wholesale Supply for the first nine months of 1976 can be summarized as follows:

Month	Sales	Net Cash Flow	Cumulative Borrowing	Ending Cash Balance
December	$20,000		$ 0	$15,000
January	30,000	($ 7,000)		
February	30,000	(4,000)		
March	40,000	(7,000)		
April	50,000	6,000		
May	40,000	23,000		
June	30,000	16,000		
July	20,000	8,000		
August	20,000	(2,000)		
September	16,000	(2,000)		

49. Net Cash Flow | $ 8,000 | ($2,000) | ($2,000)
Borrow (Repay) | 0 | 0 | 0
Ending Cash Balance | $50,000 | $48,000 | $46,000
Cumulative Borrowing | 0 | 0 | 0

Their peak borrowing need is reached in March, and they are able to start paying the loan back in April. The short term loan is expected to be completely paid off by the end of _____ . Since the fund needs do appear to be temporary, the company should have little difficulty in arranging temporary financing if it is in otherwise sound financial shape. Lenders will consider the company a better risk if needs are recognized in advance, and management can benefit from planning ahead for fund needs.

51. The basics of preparing a cash budget have now been covered. As can be seen, the cash budget is a very useful tool for planning short term fund needs. The ability to look ahead and foresee borrowing needs allows the company to plan for the acquisition of funds under conditions other than panic.

52. The cash budget is also interesting as a method for studying and illustrating the effect of sales on cash flows. You will note that cash outflows tended to precede sales and cash inflows tended to *precede / lag behind* sales. The manager cannot, therefore, count on an increase in sales to provide necessary cash for operations. Increased sales, if anything, will provide increased demands for cash over the short run.

F. CURRENT LIABILITIES

53. Having completed the analysis of current assets, the remaining area of working capital management to be covered is the effect of current asset

50. Month	Ending Cash Balance	Cumulative Borrowing	52. *lag behind*
January	$ 8,000	$ 0	
February	8,000	4,000	
March	8,000	11,000	
April	8,000	5,000	
May	26,000	0	
June	42,000	0	
July	50,000	0	
August	48,000	0	
September	46,000	0	

May

management and other factors on the current liability policy of the firm. The firm must decide what portion of assets are to be financed with current liabilities and which particular current liabilities are to be used.

54. The general guiding rule in deciding what portion of total assets should be financed by current liabilities is that assets should not be financed in such a way that payment is likely to fall due sooner than the assets can be liquidated. This would mean that current liabilities should not exceed current assets. Beyond this, however, a considerable portion of current assets are "permanent" in the sense that they are not expected to fall below a certain level as long as the business continues to operate, and could not be easily liquidated in a business downturn. Current liabilities could, however, decline quite rapidly during a business downturn. For example, a decline in sales will leave the company with considerable inventory but with accounts payable generated by inventory purchases coming due. In a sales downturn the company may have considerable difficulty in liquidating inventory to pay accounts payable. In the same manner, short term bank loans used to finance inventory may come due at a time when inventory cannot be liquidated. Recognizing the above factors, a frequent rule of thumb is that the acid test ratio should not be less than 1.0. Since inventory is the most difficult asset to liquidate in times of financial stress, a 1.0 acid test ratio limit indicates that the remaining current assets besides inventory equal or exceed the current liabilities. These are the items which the company can be reasonably confident of liquidating under conditions of stress. Another rule of thumb is that current liabilities should not be over 1/2 of total current assets. In other words, the company should not have a current ratio of less than 2.0. This guideline is supposed to provide a reasonable cushion during business fluctuations.

55. Refer to the financial statements of Office Supply Corporation presented in Chapter 1. Fill in their current ratios and acid test ratios below:

	1973	1974	1975
Acid Test Ratio	_____	_____	_____
Current Ratio	_____	_____	_____

In 1975, their current ratio and acid test ratio were both above that considered a safe minimum by the above mentioned guidelines. In fact, they could have increased current liabilities to $_____ before reaching a current ratio of 2.0. At that point, they would still have had an acid test ratio of _____ .

56. Office Supply's 1974 current ratio fell below the guideline figure of 2.0. To achieve a current ratio of 2.0, current liabilities for 1974 would have had to be reduced to $_____ .

Skip to Frame 59 if you got the correct answer.

57. To achieve a 2.0 current ratio for 1974, current liabilities should have been reduced to 1/2 of current assets of 50/2 = $25. At that level of current liabilities, the acid test ratio would have been raised to a comfortable _____ .

58. In 1973, they could have increased current liabilities to _____ before reaching the limit on acid test ratio but any increase in current liabilities would have brought the current ratio below 2.0.

59. Other factors to be considered in computing an acceptable level of current liabilities are the stability of the business and the proportion of current liabilities likely to come due under adverse conditions. The seasonal nature of the business is also important. For example, Powell Wholesale (Frame 50) might temporarily fall below its normal standards on current ratio and acid test ratio during the peak fund month of _____ .

60. The choice of which sources of temporary funds to use depends on both the cost and the expected availability of funds from that source under conditions of stress. A loan from a bank with a reputation for demanding instant payment on any sign of temporary financial difficulty would increase risks and require additional adjustment in terms of a higher than normal current ratio and acid test ratio.

61. The two primary sources of short term financing are trade credit, or accounts payable, and short term bank loans. As shown in Frame 22 to 27 of this chapter, the use of the full term available through trade credit can

---

55.	Acid Test Ratio	1.20	1.00	1.50	57. $30/25 = 1.2$
	Current Ratio	2.00	1.67	2.25	58. $24
	$45				
	60/45 = 1.33				59. March
56.	$25				

frequently be an expensive source of funds. However, the borrower should also be aware of certain adjustments which make other loans more expensive than the stated rate of interest might indicate.

62. Two frequently followed practices which raise the cost of borrowing are compensating balances and discounting of interest. Amtec arranges for a $100,000 one year loan from its bank. The bank's stated interest rate is 8% but the bank discounts the interest in advance. Amtec, therefore, receives only $100,000 − .08($100,000) = $_____. Amtec must then repay the full $100,000 at the end of the year; they actually pay $8,000 for the use of $92,000 or an interest rate of $8,000/$92,000 = _____ %.

63. School Product Corporation needs $1,000 for a period of one year. One bank is willing to loan them the money at 9.5%. Another bank will loan them the money at 9% but discounts the interest in advance. The 9% discounted loan actually costs them _____ % per year. Therefore, the _____ % loan is the lower cost loan.

Skip to Frame 65 if you got the correct answer.

64. A 10% loan with interest discounted in advance is equivalent to a _____ % loan without interest discounted in advance.

65. The other practice which raises interest rates is the compensating balance requirement. Under a compensating balance arrangement, the bank requires the borrower to maintain a demand deposit balance equal to a certain percent of the value of the loan. If the company would not otherwise have maintained the balance, the effect is to require the company to pay interest on more money than it actually has to use.

66. A particular bank charges 8% interest but requires a 20% compensating balance. If a customer borrows $1,000, he will actually only have $1,000 − .20($1,000) = $_____ to use. However, the borrower will be required to pay annual interest of .08 × $1,000 = $_____. The effective interest rate is therefore 80/800 = _____ %.

---

62. $92,000   64. 10/90 = 11.1%
    8.7%
                   66. $800
63. 9.9% $80
    9.5%   10%

67. A $1,000 10% loan with a 10% compensating balance requirement is equivalent in cost to a _____% loan with no compensating balance requirement. (Note—the effective interest cost as a percent does not depend on the size of the loan. If this is not obvious to you, verify it by reworking this problem for a $10,000 loan.)

68. In choosing between alternate sources of short term funds, the main two considerations are the cost of the funds and the "loyalty" of the lender during times of temporary financial difficulty. In deciding the proportion of funds to be financed through current liabilities, the guiding rule is that current liabilities which may come due under conditions of financial stress should not exceed the value of assets that can be liquidated relatively quickly under these conditions.

SUMMARY

A. DEFINITIONS
   1. Working Capital Management: The management of the current assets and current liabilities of the firm
      a. Working Capital: Total current assets
      b. Net Working Capital: Current assets minus current liabilities
   2. Goal of Working Capital Management: Maximize the profitability of the firm while holding risk to an acceptable level.

B. INVENTORY MANAGEMENT
   1. Inventory costs
      a. Ordering costs
      b. Carrying costs, including the cost of funds invested
      c. Lost order opportunity costs

---

67. 11.1%

2. Inventory decisions
    a. Optimum order quantity $= \sqrt{(2 \times S \times O)/C}$
       where:
       S = Total demand per period, in units
       O = Ordering costs per order
       C = Carrying cost per unit per period
    b. Reorder point: The lower the reorder point, the lower the inventory carrying cost but the greater the possibility of lost sales due to insufficient inventory. The objective of reorder point policy is to minimize the sum of the inventory carrying costs and the lost order opportunity cost.

C. ACCOUNTS RECEIVABLE MANAGEMENT

1. Accounts receivable costs and profit
    a. Cost of funds tied up in accounts receivable
    b. Cost of bad debt losses
    c. Profit on additional sales attributable to credit policy
2. Accounts receivable decisions
    a. Who to grant credit to: More liberal policy generates more sales but ties up more funds and increases bad debt losses. The best policy will maximize profits.
    b. Due date: Liberal credit terms also generate more sales but increase the investment in accounts receivable. The optimum trade-off is again the goal.
    c. Prompt payment discount: A prompt payment discount frequently makes the use of the full credit term quite expensive. For example, terms of 3/10, net 30, which means that payment is due on the 30th day but a 3% discount is allowed if the bill is paid within 10 days, raise the cost of using the full term to an effective annual interest rate of $(3/97) \times 365/(30-10) = 56.4\%$.

D. CASH BUDGETING

1. Purpose: The cash budget allows the company to plan for cash needs so that it can minimize excess cash while protecting liquidity.
2. Approach: The cash budget proceeds from the sales forecast to an estimate of all cash inflows and outflows. From the cash budget, it is then possible to plan for borrowing and the investment of temporarily excess funds.

E. CURRENT LIABILITY MANAGEMENT

1. Total amount of current liabilities
   a. Guiding principle: Assets should not be financed in such a way that payment is likely to fall due sooner than the assets can be liquidated.
   b. Rule of thumb based on the guiding principle:
      1) Current ratio should not be less than 2.0
      2) Acid test ratio should not be less than 1.0
2. The mix of current liabilities
   a. Cost
      1) As shown earlier, the use of the full terms on trade credit can sometimes be quite expensive.
      2) A compensating balance requirement states that a certain percent (P) of the loan must remain on deposit in the bank. This reduces funds available and raises the true cost of the loan (r) above the stated interest rate (i) as follows:

      $r = i/ (1-P)$

      3) The discounting of interest in advance has a similar effect on the real cost of the loan. For example, a one year 8% loan with the interest discounted in advance would have a true interest cost of $8/92 = 8.7\%$
   b. Risk
      Some sources of current financing are more likely to remain available during times of financial stress. Selection of the more stable sources decreases risk and increases the amount of funds that can safely be borrowed from short term sources.

PROBLEMS

PROBLEM 1:
American Products has sales of 200,000 units per year. Inventory carrying costs are $50 per unit per year and ordering costs are $500 per order. What is the optimum order quantity?

PROBLEM 2:
Northeast Controls processes orders of 100 units during 1/2 of the months, 200 units during 1/4 of the months, and 300 units during 1/4 of

the months. Average inventory carrying costs per month at reorder points of 100, 200, and 300 units are $50, $100, and $175, respectively. Average ordering cost per month is $50 regardless of reorder point. The lost profit per unit of orders lost due to lack of inventory is $2. A reorder point of *100/200/300* will provide the lowest total inventory cost.

PROBLEM 3:

Compute the effective amount interest rate for failure to take advantage of the prompt payment discount under each of the following credit terms:
a. 2/10, net 30
b. 3/30, net 45
c. 3/30, net 90
d. 2/20, net 60

PROBLEM 4:

XYZ now sells on terms of net 30 and is considering a change to terms of net 60. XYZ is willing to make all investments with an earning power greater than 20%. The anticipated effect of the change in credit is summarized as follows:

	Net 30 (actual)	Net 60 (anticipated)	Change
Sales	$1,000	$1,200	$200
Net Operating Income	100	120	20
Accounts Receivable	82	197	115
Total Assets	500	630	130

PROBLEM 5:

XYZ (Problem 4) is considering a new group of customers. These customers would, like their present customers, buy on terms of net 30. They would buy $200 of merchandise a year and would increase net operating income, before allowing for bad debt losses, by $20. Bad debt losses from the group of customers would be 2% of sales to them. Additional accounts receivable of $17 would be generated and other assets would be increased by $33. XYZ is willing to make all investments with an earning power greater than 20%. Should they sell to this group of customers?

PROBLEM 6:

Bank A is willing to grant a one year loan at 11% interest. Bank B charges only 10% but discounts the interest in advance. For a one year loan, which bank charges the lower effective interest?

PROBLEM 7:

Bank X is willing to grant a one year loan at 8%. Bank Y charges only 6% but requires a 20% compensating balance. Which bank provides the lower cost loan?

PROBLEM 8:

Gold Coast Manufacturing collects receivables on terms of net 60. Purchases of inventory each month equal 50% of the next month's expected sales. Inventory is paid for during the month following purchase. Labor expense equals $2 per month, regardless of the sales level.

A tax payment of $1 is expected in March and a sinking fund payment of $5 is due in March. Selling and administrative expenses will average $1 per month. A plant modernization payment of $10 is due in January. An interest payment of $1 is due in March. The January 1 cash balance is $5 and there is no short term debt. The minimum cash balance is $5. The company will borrow short term against its line of credit to maintain this cash balance. Sales for the last months of 1975 and projected sales for the first half of 1976 appear below. Prepare a cash budget for the first 6 months of 1976.

Month	Sales
November	$12
December	13
January	10
February	10
March	10
April	10
May	8
June	8
July	8

SOLUTIONS

SOLUTION 1:

$$ROQ = \sqrt{(2 \times 200{,}000 \times 500)/50} = \sqrt{4{,}000{,}000} = 2{,}000 \text{ units}$$

SOLUTION 2:

Reorder Point	Order	Lost Orders	Lost Order Opportunity Cost	Probability	Expected Opportunity Cost
	100	0	0	.50	$ 0
100	200	100	200	.25	50
	300	200	400	.25	100
			Total Expected Opportunity Cost =		$150
	100	0	0	.50	$ 0
200	200	0	0	.25	0
	300	100	200	.25	50
					$ 50
	100	0	0	.50	$ 0
300	200	0	0	.25	0
	300	0	0	.25	0
					$ 0

Reorder Point	Expected Total Inventory Cost per Month
100	$50 + $50 + $150 = $250
200	$50 + $100 + $50 = $200
300	$50 + $175 + $0 = $225

The lowest expected total inventory cost per month occurs at a reorder point of 200 units.

SOLUTION 3:

2/98 × 365/ (30–10) = .0204 × 18.25 = 37.23%
3/97 × 365/(45–30) = .0309 × 24.33 = 75.18%
3/97 × 365/ (90–30) = .0309 × 6.08 = 18.79%
2/98 × 365/ (60–20) = .0204 × 9.13 = 18.63%

SOLUTION 4:

Earning power on the marginal investment equals:

$$\frac{\text{Change in net operating income}}{\text{Change in total assets}} = \frac{20}{130} = 15.4\%$$

They should *not* change to net 60 terms

SOLUTION 5:

Earning power on the marginal investment equals:

$$\frac{\text{Change in net operating income}}{\text{Change in total assets}} = \frac{16}{50} = 32\%$$

They should sell to the new group of customers

SOLUTION 6:

	Effective Interest Rate
Bank A	11%
Bank B	.10/(1 - 0.1) - 11.1%

SOLUTION 7:

	Effective Interest Rate
Bank X	8%
Bank Y	6/80 = 7.5%

SOLUTION 8:

Gold Coast Manufacturing

	Nov.	Dec.	Jan.	Feb.	Mar.	Apr.	May	June
Monthly Sales	$12	$13	$10	$10	$10	$10	$ 8	$ 8
Collection AR		12	13	10	10	10	10	
Inventory Purchases	5	5	5	5	4	4		
Payment Accounts Payable		5	5	5	5	4	4	
Direct Labor		2	2	2	2	2	2	
Tax Payment				1				
Sinking Fund Payment				5				
Selling & Admin. Exp.		1	1	1	1	1	1	
Plant Modernization		10						
Interest Payment				1				
Total Payments		18	8	15	8	7	7	
Net Cash Flow		(6)	5	(5)	2	3	3	
Beginning Cash		5	5	5	5	5	5	
Unadjusted Cash Balance		(1)	10	0	7	8	8	
Borrow (Repay)		6	(5)	5	(2)	(3)	(1)	
Ending Cash Balance	$ 5	$ 5	$ 5	$ 5	$ 5	$ 5	$ 7	
Cumulative Borrowing	$ 0	$ 6	$ 1	$ 6	$ 4	$ 1	$ 0	

5

TIME VALUE OF MONEY

There are many problems in the field of finance that involve a choice between some amount of money now and a larger amount at some time in the future. In fact, such decisions are central to most finance problems. Investment decisions involve the payment of some amount of money now with the expectation that future amounts greater than the original investment will be received. The investor must choose between numerous alternatives, each with its own patterns of expected returns. To make such a choice, it is necessary to find a way to equate amounts received at different times. Much of personal finance involves plans aimed at the accumulation of certain amounts of money at certain future times. To plan rationally, it is helpful to know what amount will be available at a future time if a particular amount is invested at the present. The purpose of this chapter is to develop the necessary tools for the analysis of such problems.

It is well known that money deposited in the bank and left to accumulate interest grows to a larger amount in the future. What you need to know is how much you will have if you leave your funds on deposit in the bank for a certain period of time. You are aware that you would not pay $100 today for the promise to deliver one hundred dollars twenty years from today. What you need to know is how much you should be willing to pay for one hundred dollars received twenty years from now. In other words, you need to know the present value of a specific amount received at a particular future time.

When you finish this chapter, you will be able to answer the following questions:

    a. If an amount of money is left to accumulate interest at a

particular interest rate for some numbers of years, how much will
it grow to by the end of the time period?

b. How much would we be willing to pay for a promise of a
particular amount of money at some date in the future if we want
to earn a particular rate of interest on our investment?

c. If we make an annual contribution for some number of years to
an account that is left to accumulate interest at a particular rate,
how much will it grow to by the end of the time period?

d. How much would we be willing to pay for a promise of a
particular amount of money each year for some number of years,
if we wish to earn a particular rate of return on our investment?

A. FUTURE VALUE OF AN INVESTMENT

1. City Bank pays 5% interest on savings accounts, compounded annually. If
you deposit $100 today, how much will you have in your account one
year from now?

Skip to Frame 3 if you got the correct answer.

2. Your account would contain the $100 you deposited plus 5% of one
hundred dollars, for a total of $105.00.

3. A formula for the solution to the problem presented in Frame 1 can be
given as:

$100 x (1 + .05) = $105.00.

This method of stating the problem and solution will prove to be useful
later on.

4. Suppose you decide to leave your money on deposit for two years instead
of one. How much would you have in your account at the end of the
second year?

Skip to Frame 6 if you got the correct answer.

---

1. $105.00

4. $110.25

5. As you will recall, you will have $105.00 on deposit at the end of the first year. Interest during the second year will be:

.05 x $105.00 = $5.25.

and the total amount on deposit at the end of the second year will be:

$105 + $5.25 = $110.25.

6. A formula for the solution to the previous problem can be given as:

$100 x $(1+ .05)^2$ = $100 x (1.1025) = $110.25.

7. Using the formula in Frame 6, determine the size of the account if it were allowed to grow for three years.

$100 x $(1 + .05)^3$ = $_____ .

8. The problem could also be set up for 20 years in the following manner:

$100 x $(1 + .05)^{20}$.

The calculations would be tedious but you could determine the amount of money that would be in your account at the end of 20 years by solving the above statement. You will soon see that the tedious portion of the calculation has been done for you.

9. With the knowledge you now have, you should (ignoring time required for calculations) be able to determine the amount you will have at the end of any number of years for any size investment and any interest rate. The solution for a beginning value of P, an interest rate of r, and n years can be written as:

P x $(1 + r)^n$.

10. Satisfy yourself that this formula will give the correct answers by using it to solve Frames 1, 4, and 7.

11. As you can see, the idea involved in interest is relatively simple. The term used to identify the type of situation described here, in which interest is paid on interest, is *compound interest*. This is the way that interest is paid on savings accounts and charged on loans.

While the idea involved is relatively simple, the calculations can quickly become very tedious. Fortunately, tables are available giving the value of

---

7. $115.76

$(1 + r)^n$ for a large variety of values of r and n. Table I on page 219 gives such information. Use this table to find the answer to Frame 7 and verify that it is the same answer you got earlier.

12. If you deposited $100 in the bank and left it for 20 years at 4% interest, how much would you have at the end of the 20 years?

Skip to Frame 14 if you got the correct answer.

13. The solution to the problem can be stated as:

$100 x $(1 + .04)^{20}$.

Going to the 20 year row and 4% column in Table I, on page 219, you find that:

$(1 + .04)^{20} = 2.191$.

The answer to Frame 12 is:

$100 x 2.191 = $219.10.

14. If you invest $2,000 in stock, and your investment grows at a compound annual rate of 8%, how much will you have at the end of ten years?

Skip to Frame 16 if you got the correct answer.

15. An 8% compound annual growth rate is the same as 8% compound interest. The problem can be solved in the following manner, using Table I:

$2,000 x $(1 + .08)^{10} = $2,000 x 2.159 = $4,318.000.

16. If you deposit $100 now, you will receive $105 a year from now. What return (interest) will you be earning?

If you missed this, look back at Frames 1 and 2 before continuing.

---

12. $219.10

14. $4,318.00

16. 5%

17. You probably solved Frame 16 by remembering that 5% interest for one year would give you $105. This is adequate for a very simple problem but will not work if $100 grew to $150 over a 20 year period and you want to know what return you earned.

A method for handling such problems can be developed by returning to the problem in Frame 16. That problem can be solved in the following manner:

   a. $105/$100 = 1.05
   b. Go to Table I and find the row for one year. Go across the row to the value closest to 1.05.
   c. This value occurs in the 5% column so you will earn 5% interest if you invest $100 today and receive $105 a year from now.

18. Use the above steps to find what return you would have earned if you had put $100 in an investment that grew to $150 over a 20 year period.

Skip to Frame 20 if you got the correct answer.

19. You should have used the following approach.
   a. 150/100 = 1.50
   b. Go to Table I and find the row for 20 years. Go across the row to the value closest to 1.50.
   c. The value closest to 1.50 is 1.486 in the 2% column so you would have earned approximately 2%.

   Verify this approach by finding what you will have if you invest $100 for 20 years at 2%.

20. Would you invest in the opportunity described in Frame 18 if the alternative was to put your money in a savings account earning 4%?

21. A "hot land deal" is advertised as an opportunity to double the value of your investment in only 10 years. If you do invest and double your money in ten years, you will have earned between _____% and _____% return on your investment.

Skip to Frame 23 if you got the correct answer.

---

18. approximately 2%   21. 6%
                                    8%
20. no

22. You should have solved this by following the same procedure outlined in Frame 17. Since the investment is expected to grow to twice its original value, the value you will be looking for in the table is *2.00*. Going across the 10 year row, you find that you will not double your investment at 6% (1.791) and will more than double it at 8% (2.159).

23. In the hot land deal described in Frame 21, suppose the advertisement promised that you could triple your money in twenty years rather than doubling it in ten. What rate of return would you earn in this case?

B. PRESENT VALUE OF A FUTURE PAYMENT

24. Since money in hand today can be invested to grow to some larger amount in the future, it follows that money received at some future date is worth less than money received today. You are holding a promise to pay $100 one year from today. You know that you can deposit money in a bank account at a 5% rate of interest. Therefore, a deposit of less than $100 today would yield $100 one year from today. For this reason, $100 received a year from now is worth less than $100. Exactly how much is the $100 one year from today worth? This problem can be solved using the same format as that suggested in the previous section of this chapter. An amount, V, could be deposited today to yield $100 one year from today, as follows:

$$V \times (1 + .05) = \$100.00.$$

From elementary algebra, you know that this is equivalent to:

$$V = \$100/(1 + .05) = \$\underline{\hspace{2cm}}.$$

Thus, the promise to pay $100 one year from today is worth no more than $95.24 today since $95.24 could be deposited and left to grow to $100 by the end of one year.

25. If the same 5% investment opportunity is available, the maximum value of a promise to pay $100 two years from today is $\underline{\hspace{2cm}}$.

The answer appears in Frame 26.

---

23. Between 5% and 6%

24. $95.24

26. The solution to frame 25 can be written as follows:

$$V = \frac{1}{(1 + .05)^2} \times \$100 = .907 \times \$100 = \underline{\$90.70}$$

27. The solution formula shown in Frame 26 is convenient because it allows a more general statement of the solution method. P is the future amount and V is the present amount or *present value*. The interest rate and number of years are represented by r and n as before.

$$V = \frac{1}{(1 + r)^n} \times P$$

Table II on page 219 contains value of $\frac{1}{(1 + r)^n}$ for numerous values of r and n.

28. Suppose you have a bill for $100 which is due ten years from now. Your bank account pays 5% interest. How much would you need to deposit today in order to have $100 ten years from now?

Skip to Frame 31 if you got the correct answer.

29. The problem can be set up as follows:

$$V = \frac{1}{(1 + .05)^{10}} \times \$100 = .614 \times \$100 = \$61.40.$$

The factor .614 was found by going to the ten year row and 5% column of Table II.

30. How much will you need to invest today at 4% in order to have $1,000 five years from now?

31. If you want to earn 5% on your investment, what is the maximum you would be willing to pay for an investment that will have a cash value of $10,000 fifteen years from today? (You will receive no dividends or other forms of cash payment prior to the time you sell the investment for $10,000.)

---

28. $61.40

30. $822.00

31. $4,810.00

32. In other words, a promise to pay $10,000 fifteen years from today is worth $_____ today if a 5% return on your investment is required. This concept is frequently stated formally as follows:

The *present value* of $10,000 received fifteen years from now, discounted at 5%, is $4,810.

33. The present value of $10,000 received fifteen years from now, discounted at 8%, is $_____. By comparing this answer with the answer to Frame 32, you will note that as the discount rate (required rate of return) increases, the present value *increases / decreases.*

34. The present value of $10,000 received thirty years from now, discounted at 8%, is $_____. By comparing this answer with the answer to Frame 33, you will note that as the time until payment increases, the present value *increases / decreases.* These relationships can be summarized in graph form as follows:

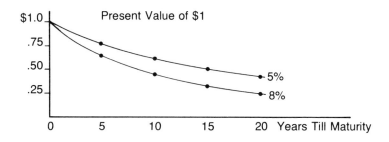

C. FUTURE VALUE OF A STREAM OF PAYMENTS

35. In this section, you will learn to find out how much you will end up with if you invest an equal amount at the end of each year for some number of years.

---

32. $4,810

33. $3,150
decreases

34. $990
decreases

36. You have decided to deposit $100 in your savings account at the *end of each year* for the next two years. The bank pays 5% interest. At the end of the first year you will make the first deposit of $_____. At the end of the second year you will make an additional deposit of $100. At the end of the second year, the first $100 will have been on deposit for one year and will have earned interest of .05 x $100 = $_____. You will therefore have a total of $100 + $100 + $5 = $_____ at the end of the second year.

37. How much would you have at the end of two years if the interest rate was 4% instead of 5%?
Follow the example presented in Frame 36, substituting 4% for 5%, if you did not get the correct answer.

38. Your savings account pays 5% interest. You decide to deposit $100 at the end of each year for the next three years. How much will you have in the account at the end of three years?

Skip to Frame 41 if you got the correct answer.

39. We can start by looking at the amount in the account at the end of the second year. This was found to be $205 in Frame 36. This $205 will be on deposit during the third year and will earn 5% interest or .05 x $205 = $_____. At the end of the third year an additional $100 is deposited for a total of:

$205 + $10.25 + $100 = $_____

40. Your savings account pays 4% interest. You decide to deposite $100 at the end of each year for the next three years. How much will you have in the account at the end of three years.

41. This type of calculation could become very tedious if done to cover ten or twenty years. This tedious calculation can be eliminated with the use of another table instead.

---

36. $100
$5
$205

37. $204

38. $315.25

39. $10.25
$315.25

40. $312.16

42. First, the solution to Frame 36 will be restated in a more formal way.

$100 + $100 × (1 + .05) = $205

Using this same formula, the solution to Frame 38 can be stated as:

$100 + $100×(1+.05) + ($100×(1+.05)^2 = $315.25.

43. This solution formula can be generalized to any number of years, n, for any interest rate, r, and any annual payment, P.

$$P + P(1 + r)^1 + P(1 + r)^2 + P(1 + r)^3 + \cdots\cdots + P(1 + r)^{n-1}$$

44. Table III on page 220 gives the values of the above mathematical statement for various values of n and r. The table, of course, is computed with P equal to $1 so that you only need to find the factor in the table and multiply by the number of dollars involved in your particular case.

45. Use Table III to solve Frames 36 and 38. Verify that these are the same answers you got through your own calculations. (Note—the answers may vary by a few cents due to rounding differences.)

46. You have decided on a savings plan which involves investing $1,000 at the end of each year for the next twenty years. If your investment earns 5%, how much will you have at the end of twenty years?

Skip to Frame 49 if you got the correct answer.

47. You should have turned to Table III on page 220 and found the intersection of the twenty year row and 5% column. At this point you will find a factor of 33.066. This is how much you would have at the end of twenty years if you saved $1.00 at the end of each year. Since you intend to save $1,000.00 each year, you would multiply by $1,000 to get 33.066 x $1,000 = *$33,066.00*

48. For the problem in Frame 46, suppose your investment earns 8% instead of 5%. How much will you have at the end of twenty years?

49. The question stated in Frame 46 can be stated in a more formal way: What is the *future value* of $1,000 invested at the end of each year for the next twenty years at 5% interest?

---

46. $33,066

48. 45.762 × $1,000 = $45,762

This is also frequently referred to as the *future value of a stream of payments* or the *future value of an annuity*.

50. What is the future value of $500 invested at the end of each year for the next ten years at 8% interest?

51. What is the future value of an annuity of $2,000 a year for fifteen years at 10% interest?

D. PRESENT VALUE OF A STREAM OF PAYMENTS

52. Your savings account pays 5% interest. How much would you need to deposit today in order to have $100 a year from today? (Solve this problem without referring to the tables.)

If you did not get the correct answer, review Section B of this chapter before continuing.

53. Your savings account pays 5% interest. How much would you deposit today in order to have $100 two years from today? (Solve this problem without referring to the tables.)

If you did not get the correct answer, review Section B of this chapter before continuing.

54. In Frame 52, you found the present value of $100 received one year from now, discounted at 5%. In Frame 53, you found the present value of $100 received two years from now, discounted at 5%. If you were asked to find the present value of $100 received at the end of each year for the next two years, discounted at 5%, you could find the answer by merely adding these two values as follows:

$$V = \frac{\$100}{(1 + .05)} + \frac{\$100}{(1 + .05)^2} = \$95.20 + \$90.70 = \underline{\underline{\$185.90}}$$

---

50. 14.487 × $500 = $7,243.50

51. 31.772 × $2,000 = $63,544

52. $100/(1+.05) = $95.20

53. $90.70

55. As we have done earlier, we will generalize this method of solution to an interest rate, r, a number of years, n, and an annual amount, P.

$$V = \frac{P}{(1+r)} + \frac{P}{(1+r)^2} + \frac{P}{(1+r)^3} + \cdots\cdots\cdots + \frac{P}{(1+r)^n}$$

56. You guessed it! There are tables available for the present value, V, based on a variety of interest rates and numbers of years. The tables, as before, are prepared for an annual payment, P, of $1.00. You only need to find the factor for the correct interest rate and number of years and then multiply by the number of dollars that are paid each year. Table IV on page 220 contains these values.

57. What is the present value of $1,000 received at the end of each year for the next ten years, discounted at 10%?

Skip to Frame 60 if you got the correct answer.

58. You should have found the present value of $1.00 at the end of each year for the next ten years, discounted at 10%, by finding the intersection of the ten year row and 10% column in Table IV. You should then have multiplied this factor by $1,000 to arrive at:

6.145 X $1,000 = $6,145.00.

59. What is the present value of $1,000 received at the end of each year for the next twenty years, discounted at 8%?

60. Your bank account pays 5% interest. You want to put enough money in the account so that you can withdraw $100 at the end of each year for the next two years. What amount will you need to deposit today?

Skip to Frame 62 if you got the correct answer.

61. This is the same as asking the present value of $100 at the end of each year for the next two years, discounted at 5%. This question was answered in Frame 54.

---

57. $6,145.00

59. $9,818.00

60. $185.90

62. Some terminology should be mentioned before leaving this section. Instead of a stream of equal payments, the word *annuity* is frequently used.

63. What is the present value of an annuity of $1,000 a year for thirty years, discounted at 10%?

E. INTEREST COMPOUNDED FOR PERIODS OTHER THAN ONE YEAR

64. The problems presented throughout this chapter have been based on annual compounding. For example, it was assumed that when money is deposited in the bank, interest is added only at the end of the year (Frames 1 and 4 for example). There are, of course, many problems where the compounding period is other than one year. For example, many banks credit interest to accounts on a quarterly, a monthly, or even a daily basis. This affects the rate at which funds grow since the depositor starts earning "interest on interest" much sooner.

65. Second National Bank has been paying interest of 8% a year on a certain type of deposit. If you deposit $1,000 in such an account, and interest is compounded annually, you will have $_____ in your account at the end of one year and $_____ at the end of two years.

Review Frames 1 to 6 of this chapter if you did not get the correct answer.

66. Second National Bank now announces a policy of compounding interest semi-annually on the 8% accounts. This means that at the end of each six months, they will credit 6 months' interest to your account. At the end of the first six months of the year, interest equal to 1/2 x .08 x $1,000 = $_____ is added to your account, bringing the total value of your account to $1,040. Interest during the second six months is then 1/2 x .08 x $1,040 = $_____. At the end of the second six months, the account will have grown to $1,040 + $41.60 = $1,081.60.

---

63. $9,427.00   66. $40.00
                                                        $41.60
65. $1,080
     $1,166.40 (or rounded to $1,166 if you used Table I)

67. You should note that $1,000 deposited for one year at 8% with interest compounded semi-annually is equivalent to $1,000 deposited for two years at an interest rate of _____ % per year. In fact, you can say in general that when money is left to grow for n years at an interest rate of r with interest compounded s times per year, it will grow to the same value as if it were allowed to grow at an interest rate of (r/s) for (n x s) years.

68. Another bank pays interest of 8% compounded quarterly. Leaving money on deposit in this bank for one year is equivalent to investing the money for four years at a _____ % interest rate. Therefore, if you left $1,000 on deposit with this bank for one year, the account would grow to $_____ .

Skip to Frame 71 if you got the correct answer.

69. Since depositing $1,000 for one year at 8% compounded quarterly is similar to depositing $1,000 for four years at 2% compounded annually, it is only necessary to go to Table I and find the factor for four years at 2%. That factor is 1.082 and your $1,000 will grow to 1.082 x $1,000 = $1,082.

70. Another bank pays interest of 10% per year, compounded semi-annually. One year at 10% is equivalent to two years at _____ %. If you deposit $100 in this bank, you will have $_____ at the end of one year.

71. Refer again to the bank that pays 8% interest, compounded quarterly. Leaving money in this account for five years is the same as investing the money for _____ years at 2%. Therefore, if you leave $1,000 on deposit for five years with this bank, your account will grow to $_____ .

Skip to Frame 74 if you got the correct answer.

---

67. 4%

68. 2%
    $1,082.43 (or rounded to $1,082 if you used Table I)

70. 5%   71. 20
    $110.20 $1,486

72. Five years at 8% compounded quarterly will give the same growth as 5 x 4 = *20* years at .08/4 = *2%*. From Table I, the factor for twenty years at 2% is 1.486. The $1,000 would therefore grow to $1,000 x 1.486 = *$1,486*.

73. You invest $100 and leave it to grow for a period of three years at an interest rate of 8% compounded quarterly. This is equivalent to allowing the money to grow for _____ years at _____% compounded annually. The $100 will grow to $_____.

74. The same approach applies when looking at the present value of a future amount. The present value of $1,000 received ten years from today, discounted at 8% compounded semi-annually, equals the present value of $1,000 received twenty years from today, discounted at 4% compounded annually. Therefore, the present value of $1,000 received ten years from today, discounted at 8% compounded semi-annually, is $_____.

75. The present value of $1,000 received five years from today, discounted at 8% compounded quarterly, is $_____.

76. The future value of a stream of payments and the present value of a stream of payments under compounding other than annually become more complex. Precise answers to problems of this type normally require the use of special tables prepared for that purpose.

SUMMARY

A. FUTURE VALUE OF A SINGLE PAYMENT

If an amount is invested at compound interest, it will grow at a rate of

$$(1 + r)^n$$

where r is the interest rate and n is the number of years the investment is

---

73. 12 years
   2%
   1.268 x 100 = $126.80

74. .456 x $1,000 = *$456*

75. .673 x $1,000 = *$673*

allowed to grow. Table I contains values of the above statement for various combinations of r and n.

B. PRESENT VALUE OF A SINGLE PAYMENT

The present value of a single payment, received n years in the future, and discounted at an interest rate of r percent, can be stated by the following equation:

$$V = P \times \frac{1}{(1 + r)^n}$$

where P equals the amount to be received in the future and V equals the present value. Values for the statement $1/(1 + r)^n$ are given in Table II for various combinations of r and n.

C. FUTURE VALUE OF STREAM OF PAYMENTS

If an amount, P, is invested at the end of each year for the next n years in an investment that earns r percent, the amount this stream of payments will grow to by the end of n years is computed as follows:

$$P + P(1 + r)^1 + P(1 + r)^2 + P(1 + r)^3 + \ldots\ldots + P(1 + r)^{n-1}$$

Table III contains values of the above statement for an annual amount of $1.00 and various combinations of r and n. It is only necessary to look up the appropriate value for the desired combination of r and n and multiply by the annual amount to be invested.

D. PRESENT VALUE OF STREAM OF PAYMENTS

The present value of an amount, P, received at the end of each year for the next n years, discounted at r percent, is computed as follows:

$$\frac{P}{(1 + r)} + \frac{P}{(1 + r)^2} + \frac{P}{(1 + r)^3} + \frac{P}{(1 + r)^4} + \ldots\ldots + \frac{P}{(1 + r)^n}$$

Table IV contains values of the above statement for an annual amount of $1.00 and various combinations of r and n. It is only necessary to look up the appropriate value for the combination of r and n and multiply by the annual amount to be received.

E. INTEREST COMPOUNDED FOR PERIODS OTHER THAN ONE YEAR

If an amount is left to grow for n years at r percent, with interest compounded s times per year, the amount will grow by the same amount as if it were left to grow for (n x s) years at (r/s) percent compounded annually. The same rule also applies to present value when interest is compounded other than annually.

PROBLEMS

PROBLEM 1:

You deposit $5,000 in your savings account. The savings account pays 6% interest. If you do not make any withdrawals, how much will be in the account at the end of ten years? How long would it take for the amount in the account to double?

PROBLEM 2:

How much would you be willing to pay for an investment that will return $500 at the end of two years, $750 at the end of three years, and can be sold for $1,000 at the end of four years if you wish to earn 8% annual interest on your investment?

PROBLEM 3:

A particular bond has a ten year life, a $1,000 face value, and a 6% nominal interest rate paid annually. In other words, the bond will pay $60 at the end of each year for the next ten years. In addition, the bond can be redeemed for $1,000 at the end of the tenth year. If you wanted to earn 8% on your investment, how much would you be willing to pay for the bond?

PROBLEM 4:

A machine will provide the following cash savings after tax. Calculate the present value of these savings, discounted at 10%. (Assume that all cash flows occur at the end of the year.)

Year	Cash Savings
1	$2,000
2	3,000
3	2,000
4	4,000

PROBLEM 5:

You want to save for an early retirement. You have an investment opportunity that will earn 10% annual return. You intend to invest $1,000 at the end of each year for the next thirty years. How much will you have at the end of thirty years?

PROBLEM 6:

Village National Bank pays interest of 4% compounded semi-annually. If you deposit $1,000 in an account at Village National and leave the money on deposit for ten years, it will grow to what amount?

SOLUTIONS

SOLUTION 1:

The first part of the problem can be stated mathematically as:

$5000 \times (1 + .06)^{10}$.

By going to the 10 year row and 6% column of Table I we find that:

$(1 + .06)^{10} = 1.791$.

The answer, therefore, is: $5,000 X 1.791 = $8,955.

Mathematically, the answer to the second part of the question is found by determining the number of years, n, for which:

$(1 + .06)^n = 2.0$.

By going down the 6% column in Table I, we discover that a value of 2.012 is found at the 12 year row. You will have slightly more than doubled your money by the end of twelve years.

SOLUTION 2:

This problem can best be solved by finding the present values of each of the three payments separately and then adding the present values together.

	Payment		Factor from Table II		Present Value
Year 2	$ 500	x	.857	=	$ 428.50
Year 3	$ 750	x	.794	=	$ 595.50
Year 4	$1000	x	.735	=	$ 735.00
		Total Present Value		=	$1759.00

If you pay *$1,759* for the investment, you will earn an 8% annual return.

SOLUTION 3:

This problem could be reworded as follows:

a. What is the present value of $60 at the end of each year for the next 10 years, discounted at 8%?

b. What is the present value of $1,000 received 10 years from now, discounted at 8%?

c. What is the sum of a and b?

The solution is as follows:

a. From the 10 year row and 8% column of Table IV, we find *6.710*.

   6.710 x $60 = $402.60

b. From the 10 year row and 8% column of Table II, we find *.463*.

   .463 x $1000 = $463.00

c. $402.60 + $463.00 = $865.60

If you pay $865 for the bond, you will earn an 8% annual return on your investment.

SOLUTION 4:

The solution to this problem is found by calculating the present value of each individual cash savings using Table II, and then summing these present values.

	Cash Savings		Factor from Table II		Present Value
Year 1	$2000	x	.909	=	$1818
Year 2	$3000	x	.826	=	$2478
Year 3	$2000	x	.751	=	$1502
Year 4	$4000	x	.683	=	$2732
	Total Present Value			=	$8530

The present value of this stream of cash savings is *$8,530*.

SOLUTION 5:

At the intersection of the 30 year row and 10% column in Table III, we find the factor 164.494. If you invest $1.00 at the end of each year for the next 30 years, you will end up with $164.494. Since you will be investing $1,000 at the end of each year, you merely multiply by $1,000.

164.494 X $1000 = $164,494.00

SOLUTION 6:

Ten years at 4% compounded semi-annually is equivalent to twenty years at 2% compounded annually. The factor from Table I for twenty years at 2% is 1.486. The deposit will therefore grow to $1,000 x 1.486 = *$1,486.*

6

CAPITAL BUDGETING

A capital investment is defined as an investment whose returns are expected to be spread over a period of more than one year. Examples of capital investments would include a drilling machine, a truck, a ship, a factory, and an apartment house. For the firm, capital investments include fixed assets as well as other investments which are expected to generate returns over extended periods of time. Capital budgeting is the process of selecting capital investments.

The success or failure of the firm can easily depend on the quality of its capital budgeting decisions. The capital assets of the firm are the productive assets. They include plant, equipment, etc., and the selection of capital assets commits the firm to particular strategies and lines of business. Furthermore, the acquisition of capital assets commits the firm to these strategies for many years. Capital assets may have lives of twenty, thirty, or more years, making it extremely difficult to reverse a decision which later proves to be unwise. For these reasons, capital budgeting decisions are frequently critical to the welfare of the firm.

Since the time commitment for fixed asset investment is considerably different than that for current assets, it is necessary to use different methods of analysis in selecting fixed assets. Since it is normally possible to liquidate current assets within a relatively limited time period if desired, it is only necessary to look at the expected return from these investments over the near term. This is accomplished by looking at the profitability effect of current asset investments. This approach is sufficient for current asset decisions but is not adequate for the evaluation of fixed assets. Fixed assets involve long term commitments with the expectation that the company will receive returns over a long period of time. In fact, many fixed asset investments will provide no returns during the first year due to start-up costs, etc. While such investments might be attractive based on their long term profitability, they would not be accepted if evaluated according to short term profitability as was done with current assets.

A method of evaluating returns spread unevenly over a number of future periods is needed for capital budgeting decisions. Such a method is available based on concepts that have been developed earlier. In the previous chapter you learned to solve many problems in which a single payment or series of payments were to be received in the future and it was necessary to find the maximum amount you would be willing to pay today. In addition to the nature of the returns expected, the primary additional information you needed was the return that could be earned from alternate investments. These techniques are applicable to capital budgeting decisions. In this case, the decision must be made from the point of view of the investors (especially common stock holders). If the present value of the stream of returns from a project, discounted at the opportunity rate available elsewhere from investments of equal risk, exceeds the cost, the project would be attractive from the company's point of view. The techniques of analyzing the returns will be further developed and refined in this chapter.

In addition to the problem of evaluating future returns, it is also necessary to determine what returns are of most interest. It is cash, and not accounting profit, which the company can use to invest in new projects, pay dividends to shareholders, etc. Therefore, it is the cash generated over the life of an investment that is of most interest, and not the profits. The analyst must be able to estimate the cash returns that will be generated by a new investment proposal. Likewise, it is the cash outlay required to acquire a new asset that is of most interest.

In this chapter, you learn to identify tax effects and other considerations to estimate the cash outlay necessary to acquire a new asset. In addition, you learn to consider the effects of these same factors in estimating the cash returns that the asset will provide. Finally, you learn to evaluate the expected cash outlay and cash return to select among capital investments available, based on the other opportunities available to investors.

A. PRESENT VALUE

1. In the previous chapter, you learned to find the present value of a stream of payments. It would be appropriate to start this chapter with a brief review

of the problem. Northwestern Corp. is considering a new capital investment. The investment will provide cash flows of $10,000 a year for 20 years. Investment opportunities of equal risk are available at an annual return of 10%. The present value of the cash flows from this investment is $_____ .

Skip to Frame 3 if you got the correct answer.

2. This problem can be restated using the terminology of the previous chapter: Find the present value of a stream of payments of $10,000 a year for 20 years, discounted at 10%. By going to the 20 year row and 10% column of Table IV, a factor of 8.514 can be found. The answer can be found as follows:

8.514 × $10,000 = $85,140.

A brief review of the previous chapter is in order if this technique and the reason for it are not perfectly clear.

3. At this point, it will be helpful to introduce some standard terminology of capital budgeting. The discount rate, or required rate of return is normally referred to as the *cost of capital*. The main determinants of the cost of capital are the returns available on alternative investment opportunities and the level of risk. These concepts and techniques for estimating the cost of capital will be developed in the following chapters.

4. When evaluating capital budgeting alternatives, it is necessary to identify the cash flows associated with various alternatives. To do this, recognition of the tax effects of various decisions is required. In the latter part of this chapter, the methods of adjusting for taxes and identifying cash flows will be treated. For the time being, it will be assumed that such adjustments have been made and the term *after-tax cash flows* will be used frequently.

5. The problem presented in Frame 1 of this chapter can now be rewritten as follows: Northwestern Corporation is considering a new capital invest-

---

1. $85,140

5. after-tax cash flows
   cost of capital

ment. The investment will provide _____ _____ _____
_____ of $10,000 a year for 20 years. Northwestern Corporation's
_____ ___ _____ is 10%.

Reread Frames 3 and 4 if you did not get the correct answer.

6. You have now been presented with the basic methods and terminology for present-value analysis. This technique will now be used to make a capital budgeting decision.

7. Refer again to the problem in Frame 5. The proposed investment will cost $70,000 and Northwestern Corporation has the $70,000 available. Should they invest in this project? _____

Skip to Frame 10 if you got the correct answer.

8. If the present value of the cash inflows provided by the project exceeds the cost, the project would be considered attractive. In this case, the present value of the cash inflows is expected to be $85,140, and the cost is $70,000 so the project would be attractive.

9. ABC Corporation is considering a capital investment. The investment will cost $7,000 and will provide after-tax cash flows of $1,000 a year for 10 years. ABC's cost of capital is 8%. The present value of the cash inflows is $_____. The present value *exceeds / does not exceed* the cost. Therefore, the project *is / is not* attractive.

10. Present value provides a gauge of the maximum amount you would be willing to pay for a particular investment. The value of the investment equals the present value of the after-tax cash flows.

11. A capital investment opportunity will provide after-tax cash flows of $10,000 a year for 5 years. If your cost of capital is 10%, the investment is worth $_____.

Skip to Frame 13 if you got the correct answer.

---

7. yes   11. $37,910

9. $6,710
   does not exceed
   is not

12. Using Table IV, you can compute the present value by the following method:

    3.791 × $10,000 = $37,910.

    Since this indicates the present value of the stream of payments, and since the value of the investment is determined by the present value of the stream of payments, the value of this investment is $_____.

13. An investment will cost $10,000. It will provide after-tax cash flows of $2,000 a year for 10 years. The cost of capital is 10%. The value of the investment equals the present value of the cash inflows, or $_____. The value of the investment exceeds its cost by $_____.

14. You have now been presented with the basic techniques of present value analysis. This section can be completed with a summary problem.

15. New Corporation is considering a capital investment project. The project will cost $20,000 and will provide after-tax cash flows of $5,000 a year for 6 years. New Corporation's cost of capital is 12%. The present value of the cash inflows is $_____. The present value *does / does not* exceed the cost. Therefore, the project *is / is not* attractive.

    If you did not get the correct answer, reread this chapter starting with Frame 3.

B. NET PRESENT VALUE

16. As you will recall, the present value of the after-tax cash flows from a project is a measure of what you would be willing to pay for the investment. If the present value exceeds the cost, it could be said that you have increased your wealth since the value of the investment is greater than the cost.

---

12. $37,910

13. $12,290
    $ 2,290

15. $20,555
    does
    is

17. For the project presented in Frame 15, the present value is $ _____ and the cost is $ _____. Therefore, it could be said that acquisition of this project would increase your wealth by $ _____.

Skip to Frame 20 if you got the correct answer.

18. The present value and cost are transferred directly from the answers in Frame 15. The increase in wealth is computed by subtracting the cost from the present value of the cash inflows as follows:

$20,555 – $20,000 = $555.

Review Frames 10 through 13 before continuing.

19. What would have been the increase in wealth if the project had cost $18,000? $_____

20. By the same token, a project that costs more than the present value of its expected cash inflows will decrease the wealth of the company or individual making the investment.

21. Refer back to the problem presented in Frame 15. If the project had cost $25,000, the cost would have exceeded the present value by $25,000 – $20,5555 = $_____, and the project would have decreased New Corporation's wealth by $_____. Therefore, the project *would / would not* be attractive.

Skip to Frame 24 if you got the correct answer.

22. Since the cost exceeds the present value by $4,445, you will be paying $4,445 more than the value of the project if you decide to invest in it. This would decrease your wealth by $4,445.

---

17. $20,555
    $20,000
    $555

19. $2,555

21. $4,445
    $4,445
    would not

23. Another project costs $30,000 and would produce after-tax cash flows with a present value of $25,000. Acceptance of this project would decrease the firm's wealth by $_____.

24. We can now introduce the definition of net present value. The *net present value* of a project is the present value of the cash inflows minus the cost.

25. A project will cost $15,000 and will provide after-tax cash flows with a present value of $18,000. The net present value of the project is $_____.

If you missed the answer to this problem, refer back to the definition of net present value in Frame 24.

26. An investment with a present value exceeding its cost will have a net present value of greater than zero. An investment with a present value less than its cost will have a net present value *greater / less* than zero.

Skip to Frame 28 if you got the correct answer.

27. The following example should clarify the point. An investment costs $10,000 and produces after-tax cash flows with a present value of $8,000. The net present value is computed as follows:

Present value	$ 8,000
−Cost	10,000
= Net present value	−2,000

28. The net present value, therefore, would indicate the change in wealth caused by selection of a particular investment. Companies will attempt to choose projects with *positive / negative* net present values.

29. If the company were not faced with a shortage of funds or some other restriction, it could maximize its worth by accepting all capital investments with a *positive / negative* net present value. It would reject all investments with a *positive / negative* net present value.

---

23. $5,000

25. $3,000

26. less

28. positive

29. positive
  negative

30. Allied Corporation is considering a capital investment which will cost $20,000 and will produce after-tax cash flows of $5,000 a year for 6 years. Allied Corporation has a 10% cost of capital. Compute the present value of the cash inflows and the net present value of the investment.

Skip to Frame 33 if you got the correct answer.

31. Going to Table IV on page 220, the intersection of the 10% column and the 6 year row produces a present value factor of 4.355.

Present value = 4.355 × $5,000 = $21,775.

Net present value = $21,775 − $20,000 = $1,775.

If your difficulty was with the computation of present value, review Section A of this chapter. If your difficulty was with conversion from present value to net present value, begin your review at Frame 16.

32. Consolidated Corporation has a 10% cost of capital. They are considering a project which will cost $8,000 and will produce after-tax cash flows of $1,000 a year for 20 years. Compute the present value and net present value.

C. PROFITABILITY INDEX

33. A decision maker would normally be interested in creating the *maximum / minimum* net present value for each dollar invested.

Skip to Frame 35 if you got the correct answer.

34. As you recall from the previous section, we concluded that positive net present value is desired. Therefore, it would seem only logical that if some net present value is good, more net present value is better. Larger net present value would cause a greater increase in total wealth. Therefore you

---

30. Present value = $21,775
    Net present value = $1,775

33. Maximum

32. Present value = $8,514
    Net present value = $514

would maximize wealth by choosing projects in such a way as to
_____ net present value. This, of course, would imply
maximization of net present value for each dollar invested.

35. The projects with the highest ratio of net present value to cost would have
the *highest / lowest* ratios of present value to cost.

Skip to Frame 37 if you got the correct answer.

36. Perhaps an example will help clarify this last point. Consider two projects,
A and B.

Project	A	B
Cost	$10,000	$10,000
Present value	12,000	13,000
Net present value	2,000	3,000
Net present value ÷ cost	.2	.3
Present value ÷ cost	1.2	1.3

Project B obviously has both a higher ratio of net present value to cost and
present value to cost. This project creates more net present value for each
dollar invested than does project A. It is therefore more desirable.

37. The ratio of present value to cost is referred to as the *profitability index.*

38. A project or investment with a present value greater than its cost will have
a profitability index *greater / less* than 1.0. An investment with a present
value less than its cost will have a profitability index *greater / less* than 1.0.

Skip to Frame 40 if you got the correct answer.

39. Again, a numerical example may be helpful. Projects X and Y are
presented below.

Project	X	Y
Present Value	$6,000	$4,000
Cost	$5,000	$5,000
Profitability Index	1.2	0.8

---

34. Maximize   **35.** Highest   **38.** greater
                                                              less

40. One last problem will suffice to complete this section. A project has a cost of $10,000 and a net present value of $1,000. The profitability index is

_____.

Skip to Frame 43 if you got the correct answer.

41. You will recall that the net present value equals present value minus cost. Therefore, for the project described in Frame 40, we know that:

Net present value = present value − cost
$1,000   = present value − $10,000
$11,000   = present value
Profitability index = $11,000/$10,000 = 1.1

42. ABC Corp. is considering a capital investment. The project will cost $20,000 and will have a net present value of $4,000. The profitability index is _____.

D. INTERNAL RATE OF RETURN

43. The *internal rate of return* is the annual compounded rate of return that would be earned from investment in a particular asset. Stated in another way, the internal rate of return is the discount factor which will make the present value equal to the cost of a project. A project is normally considered attractive if its internal rate of return exceeds its cost of capital.

44. If you invest $100 in a project that will return $105 a year from today, you will earn a _____% return on your investment.

45. If you invest $95.20 in a project that will return $100 one year from now, you will earn _____% return on your investment.

46. The simplest way to find the answer to this question is to turn to Table II and go across the one year row until you find the present value factor which when multiplied by $100 equals $95.20. This factor, of course, is .952 found at the 5% column.

---

40. 1.1   **44.** 5%

42. 1.2   **45.** 5%

47. If you invest $55.80 in a project that will return $100 ten years from now, you will earn an annual return of _____ %.

Skip to Frame 50 if you got the correct answer.

48. You can find the answer to 47 by the same method you used to find the answer to 45. Go across the ten year row of Table II until you find a present value factor that will make the present value of $100 equal to $55.80. This factor is found at the _____ % column.

49. If you invest $38.60 in a project that will return $100 ten years from today, you will earn an annual return of _____ %.

50. If you invest $185.90 in a project that will return $100 at the end of each year for the next two years, you will earn _____ % return on your investment.

Skip to Frame 52 if you got the correct answer.

51. You can find the answer to this problem by going to Table IV and finding the present value factor that will make the present value of $100 at the end of each year for the next 2 years equal to $185.90. This factor is found at the _____ % column.

52. In other words, the project described in Frame 50 has an internal rate of return equal to _____ %.

53. Finding the internal rate of return for a complex problem is the same as that described for the simple problems above. You simply solve for the present value using various discount rates until you find the discount rate that yields a present value closest to the cost of the project.

---

47. 6%

48. 6%

49. 10%

50. 5%

51. 5%

52. 5%

54. A project costs $3,312 and provides the after-tax cash flows shown below. Find the internal rate of return.

Year	After-tax Cash Flows
1	$1,000
2	2,000
3	1,000

Skip to Frame 57 if you got the correct answer.

55. The answer is found by a trial-and-error process of solving for the present value of the cash flows at various discount rates. At a 10% discount rate, the present value of the cash flows equals $3,312.

56. A project costs $4,007 and provides the after-tax cash flows shown below. Find the internal rate of return.

Year	After-tax Cash Flows
1	$2,000
2	1,000
3	2,000

57. For most problems, you will not find a discount rate that will make the present value of the cash flows exactly equal to the cost. In those cases, you will have to settle for an approximate internal rate of return.

58. A project costs $2,600 and will provide the after-tax cash flows outlined below. The internal rate of return is between _____% and _____%.

Year	After-tax Cash Flows
1	$1,000
2	2,000

Skip to Frame 61 if you got the correct answer.

---

54. 10%   58. 8%   10%

56. 12%

59. At a 10% discount rate, the present value is $2,561 and at an 8% discount rate the present value is $2,640. Therefore, a discount rate between 8% and 10% will provide a present value of $2,600.

60. If the cost of the project described in Frame 58 was $2,500, the internal rate of return would be between _____ % and _____ %.

61. Some authors use the term *discounted rate of return* instead of internal rate of return. Therefore, internal rate of return means the same thing as

_____ _____ _____ _____ .

E. PAYBACK PERIOD

62. While present value analysis is the primary method of evaluating capital budgeting proposals in modern business, the payback period is also of interest in some cases.

63. The *payback period* is the number of years it takes for the cash inflows generated by a capital investment to equal its cost.

64. The payback period is more a measure of liquidity than a measure of profitability. As a measure of how long it takes to recover the initial investment, the payback period is of interest to a company for which early recovery is seen as critical. It is also seen as giving some indication of risk since uncertainty increases with time. Its quality as a risk indicator is, however, limited by the fact that there are many very risky projects with short payback periods and many relatively safe projects with long payback periods.

65. A project costs $10,000 and will product after-tax cash flows of $5,000 a year for three years. The payback period is _____ years.

Skip to Frame 67 if you got the correct answer.

66. Since the project generates $5,000 in cash flows each year, it will generate $10,000 in cash flows over a two year period. Therefore, the original $10,000 cost will have been recovered in two years.

---

60. 10%,   12%

61. discounted rate of return

65. 2

67. Another project costs $10,000 and will produce after-tax cash flows of $4,000 a year for 4 years. The payback period is _____ years.

Skip to Frame 70 if you got the correct answer.

68. The project will produce cash flows of $4,000 in the first year and $4,000 in the second year for a total of $8,000 in the first two years. It will require all of these first two years' cash flows plus half of an additional year's cash flows for a total of *2½ years'* cash flows.

69. A project will cost $14,000 and will produce after-tax cash flows of $4,000 a year for six years. The payback period is _____ years.

70. A project will cost $10,000 and will produce after-tax cash flows of $3,000 a year for five years. The payback period is _____ years.

F. PROJECT SELECTION

71. In the previous sections of this chapter, several conclusions about the attractiveness of potential capital investment projects were drawn. For example, a capital investment project is desirable if the present value of the cash flows from the project is *greater* / *less* than the cost, or the profitability index is *greater* / *less* than 1.0.

72. It was also decided that a project is attractive if the net present value is *greater* / *less* than zero or the internal rate of return is *greater* / *less* than the cost of capital.

---

67. 2½

69. 3½

70. 3 1/3

71. greater
    greater

72. greater
    greater

73. If a capital investment has a present value greater than its cost, it will also have a profitability index greater than 1.0, a net present value greater than zero and an internal rate of return *greater* / *less* than the cost of capital.

74. Therefore, a project which is attractive according to present value analysis *is* / *is not* attractive according to these other methods of analysis. Likewise, a project which is unattractive when evaluated with one method, will also be unattractive when evaluated according to the others.

75. Therefore, if a company is able to invest in all attractive projects, it *does* / *does not* make a difference which of these methods of analysis is used.

76. A problem arises when the company cannot invest in all attractive projects which are available. There may be numerous attractive projects available at a time when the company has limited funds available. The company may also have opportunities which are mutually exclusive, such as the choice between two methods of production.

77. American Products, with a 10% cost of capital, must make a choice between two machines. Machine A has a net present value of $10,000 and an internal rate of return of 15%. Machine B has a net present value of $13,000 and an internal rate of return of 12%. Why is one project more attractive when evaluated according to net present value and the other more attractive when evaluated according to internal rate of return? This difference is caused by the reinvestment assumptions implicit in the internal rate of return and net present value calculations. The internal rate of return method is based on the assumption that all cash flows from the project can be reinvested at the internal rate of return while the net present value method is based on the assumption that cash flows can be reinvested at the cost of capital. Since the cost of capital is based on alternative investment opportunities, it is generally felt that the maximization of net present value is the most suitable goal in these situations. Maximization of net present value is consistent with the earlier stated goal of maximizing owners' wealth. American Products should therefore choose machine _____ .

---

73. greater   75. does not

74. is   77. B

142

Capital Budgeting

78. Allied Products Corporation has only enough funds to invest in one of the two projects below. They should invest in project _____.

Project	Net Present Value	Internal Rate of Return
A	$20,000	18%
B	25,000	14%

79. Allied Corporation has only $20,000 to invest during the coming year. They have the following projects to choose from. Which projects should they select?

Project	Cost	Net Present Value	Internal Rate of Return
A	$10,000	$1,500	14%
B	$10,000	$2,000	16%
C	$10,000	$2,500	12%

Skip to Frame 81 if you got the correct answer.

80. Projects B and C in Frame 79 will produce a net present value of $4,500. As they can only choose two projects with the budget limitations they face, this is the maximum net present value they can achieve. The second best alternative would be projects A and C with a total net present value of $4,000.

81. Consolidated Corporation has the following capital investments to choose from. They have a total of $22,000 available to invest. Which projects should they select?

Project	Cost	Net Present Value
A	$10,000	$2,000
B	$20,000	$3,500
C	$10,000	$1,800

---

78. B   **81.** A and C

79. B and C

Skip to Frame 85 if you got the correct answer.

82. All of the projects have positive net present values and would be attractive. However, with only $22,000 to invest they can choose either B alone or A and C. Choice of B alone would provide $3,500 in net present value and choice of A and C would provide $3,800 in net present value.

83. A company has the following projects to choose from. They have $20,000 to invest. Which projects should they choose?

Project	Cost	Net Present Value
A	$9,000	$2,000
B	$20,000	$3,000
C	$10,000	$2,000

Skip to Frame 85 if you got the correct answer.

84. Project B chosen alone would exhaust their resources and produce a net present value of $3,000. Projects A and C would not fully exhaust their resources but would not leave enough funds to choose another project. By choosing A and C they can create a net present value of $4,000. Concern is frequently expressed about the uninvested $1,000 since the costs of projects A and C total only $19,000. The company can use these funds for such activities as repayment of debt, repurchase of common stock, or payment of dividends.

85. A company has the following projects to choose from. They have $30,000 to invest. Which projects should they choose?

Project	Cost	Present Value	Net Present Value
A	$9,000	$11,000	
B	$8,000	$10,000	
C	$10,000	$11,500	
D	$11,000	$12,000	

Skip to Frame 88 if you got the correct answer.

---

83. A and C   85. A, B, and C

86. Note that the present values were given rather than the net present values. If you chose in such a way as to maximize present value rather than net present value, you would have arrived at an incorrect answer. Projects A, B, and C would create a total net present value of $5,500. No other possible combination would produce as much net present value.

87. A company has the following projects to choose from. They have $10,000 to invest. Which projects should they choose?

Project	Cost	Present Value
A	$3,000	$3,500
B	$4,000	$4,200
C	$3,000	$3,300
D	$2,500	$3,000

G. IDENTIFICATION OF CASH FLOWS

88. In all of the previous problems cash flows have been given. You will now learn how to find these cash flows. The first step is to identify the cash outlay connected with the acquisition of a capital investment. For a capital investment project such as a piece of machinery, the initial outlay is an investment rather than an expense for tax purposes. Therefore, there are no tax considerations and the cash flow, net of tax effects (frequently referred to as the *after-tax cash flow*) to acquire the investment will directly equal the cost.

89. A machine will cost $10,000. If the company purchasing the machine is facing a 48% marginal tax rate, the cash flow net of tax considerations necessary to acquire the machine will be $_____.

Refer again to Frame 88 if you did not get the correct answer.

90. The next step is to consider the effect of taxes on income. After-tax cash flows will normally be computed by adjusting before-tax profits for tax effects.

---

87. A, C, and D   89. $10,000

91. The plant manager for Associated Widget developed a new processing method that would cost nothing to install but would decrease labor expenses by $100,000 a year. If Associated Widget faces a 48% marginal tax rate the cash flows from this investment will equal $_____ a year.

Skip to Frame 94 if you got the correct answer.

92. Since labor expenses will decrease by $100,000, profit before tax will increase by $100,000 and taxes will increase by $48,000. After-tax cash flows will therefore increase by:

$100,000 − $48,000 = $52,000.

93. Southeastern Corporation has developed a new process which will decrease materials waste by $10,000 a year. The company faces a 48% marginal tax rate. The annual after-tax cash savings from this new process will be $_____ .

94. Depreciation is not a cash expense but it is of interest to us because it decreases reportable income and therefore decreases taxes payable.

95. A machine will cost $10,000. It will have a four year life and zero salvage value at the end of the four years. Based on this estimated life and terminal value, annual depreciation would be (10,000 − 0)/4 = $_____ using the straight line method.

96. The machine discussed in Frame 95 will reduce labor expense by $3,500 a year. The company faces a 48% marginal tax rate. Purchase of this machine will increase profit before tax by the amount of labor savings minus depreciation or $_____ . Taxes will be increased by the amount of:

.48 × profit before tax = $_____ .

Annual after-tax cash flows will be increased by:

labor savings − taxes = $_____ .

---

91. $52,000

93. $5,200

95. $2,500

96. $1,000
$480
$3,020

97. The solution to the previous problem, and a general format for the solution of similar problems, can be summarized as follows:

	Income Items	Cash Flow Items
Labor Savings	$3,500	$3,500
Increased Depreciation	2,500	
Increased Profit Before Tax	1,000	
Increased Tax	480	480
Increased Profit After Tax	$520	
Increased After-tax Cash Flow		$3,020

98. Omega Corporation is considering a new automatic drill press. The drill press will cost $50,000. It has a five year life and a zero salvage value. The machine will reduce labor expense by $12,000 a year. Omega Corporation faces a 48% marginal tax rate. What will be the annual after-tax cash flows generated by the machine?

Annual depreciation (straight line) = $_____.

	Income Items	Cash Flow Items
Labor Savings	$	$
Increased Depreciation		
Increased Profit Before Tax	_____	
Increased Tax	_____	_____
Increased Profit After Tax	_____	
Increased After-tax Cash Flows		_____

98.
Annual depreciation	$10,000
Labor Savings	12,000
Increased Profit Before Tax	2,000
Increased Tax	960
Increased Profit After Tax	1,040
Increased After-tax Cash Flows	11,040

99. Allied Corporation is considering a new machine. The machine would cost $100,000. It would have a five year life and a zero salvage value. The machine would increase profits before depreciation and taxes by $25,000 a year. Allied will use the straight line depreciation method and it faces a 48% marginal tax rate. What would be the annual after-tax cash flow generated by the machine?

Skip to Frame 102 if you got the correct answer.

100. Annual depreciation would be $100,000/5 = $20,000. Annual after-tax cash flows can then be computed as follows:

	Income Items	Cash Flow Items
Increased Profits Before Tax and Depreciation	$25,000	$25,000
Increased Depreciation	20,000	
Increased Profit Before Tax	5,000	
Increased Tax	2,400	2,400
Increased Profit After Tax	$2,600	
Increased After-tax Cash Flow		$22,600

101. Normal Corporation is considering the purchase of a new fork-lift truck. The truck will cost $36,000 and will last for six years. The truck will have a zero salvage value at the end of six years. It will replace one worker, whose annual salary and connected benefits are $7,000 a year. Normal Corporation uses straight line depreciation and faces a 48% marginal tax rate. The purchase of a fork-life truck would result in an increase in annual after-tax cash flows of $_____ .

102. You have now dealt with the initial cost and annual cash flows from a capital investment. We will now consider tax implications of the sale of a capital investment.

---

99. $22,600

100. $6,520

103. If a depreciated capital asset is sold at its book value, the cash from the sale is recognized as a return of capital. Since the original purchase was not an expense for tax purposes, the sale of the asset is not treated as income for tax purposes. Therefore, if an asset with a book value of $5,000 is sold for $5,000, the after-tax cash flow recognized from the sale would be $_____.

Skip to Frame 105 if you got the correct answer.

104. From the earlier part of Frame 103, you will note that a sale at book value receives no tax treatment. Therefore, a sale of a capital asset for $5,000 will not increase the company's tax payment and will result in a cash flow of $5,000.

105. The problem becomes somewhat more complex when a capital asset is sold for a price different than its depreciated book value. Some illustrative rules covering such sales can be summarized as follows:
  a. If the asset is sold above its depreciated book value but not above its original cost, the difference is taxed as ordinary income.
  b. If the asset is sold for less than its book value, the difference is treated as an expense for tax purposes and results in a tax savings equal to the company's marginal tax rate times that loss if there is a sufficient tax liability against which to offset the loss.
These rules will be illustrated in the following frames.

106. An asset originally cost $10,000. It has been depreciated to a book value of $5,000. The asset is then sold for $6,000. There is a $1,000 gain on this sale, and the gain is taxed at the corporation's ordinary income tax rate of 48%. Taxes due on the sale will be $1,000 × .48 = $_____ and after-tax cash proceeds will be $6,000 − $480 = $_____ .

107. Allied Corporation sells a capital asset for $4,000. The asset originally cost $5,000 and had been depreciated to a book value of $2,000. The company faces a 48% marginal tax rate. Taxes on the sale will be $_____, and after-tax cash proceeds from the sale will be $_____.

Skip to Frame 110 if you got the correct answer.

---

103. $5,000

106. $480
     $5,520

107. $960
     $3,040

108. Allied Corporation will pay taxes equal to 48% of the difference between the sale price and the book value. Since this difference is $2,000, the tax payable will be $960. After-tax cash proceeds will be $4,000 − $960 = $3,040.

109. American Corporation sells an asset for $10,000. The asset had an original cost of $15,000 and had been depreciated to a book value of $8,000. The corporation faces a 48% marginal tax rate. Taxes on the sale of the asset would be $_____, and after-tax cash proceeds from the sale would be $_____.

110. American Corporation has a machine which is no longer needed. The machine has a book value of $50,000 but can be sold for only $30,000. American is expected to have total profit before tax of $200,000 for the year and faces a 48% marginal tax rate on regular income. Since it has sufficient profits against which the loss on the sale can be offset, it will recognize a tax savings through the sale. The difference between the book value and the sale price is $_____. Since this amount is a loss, it will result in a tax savings of .48 × $20,000 = $_____. The after-tax cash proceeds from the sale will be the $30,000 sale price plus the $9,600 tax savings for a total of $_____.

111. ABC Corporation has a surplus conveyor. The original cost of the conveyer was $30,000 and it can be sold for $12,000. The book value of the conveyer is now $20,000. The corporation has sufficient income from other sources to take advantage of any tax savings. It face a 48% tax rate on regular income and a 25% rate on capital gains. The tax savings from the sale of the machine would be $_____, and the after-tax cash proceeds would be $_____.

Skip to Frame 114 if you got the correct answer.

---

109. $960
$9,040

110. $20,000
$ 9,600
$39,600

111. $ 3,840
$15,840

112. The amount subject to tax treatment was the difference between the book value and the sale price, or $8,000. The tax savings would be .48 X $8,000 = $3,840, and the after-tax cash proceeds would be the sale price plus the tax savings, or $12,000 + $3,840 = $15,840.

113. American Service Corp. is considering the sale of a truck. It paid $12,000 for the truck which now has a book value of $10,000 and could be sold for $8,000. The corporation faces a tax rate of 48% on regular income and 30% on capital gains. Tax savings from sale of the truck would be $_____, and after-tax cash proceeds from the sale would be $_____ .

Return to Frame 110 if you did not get the correct answer.

114. It should be pointed out the tax laws applicable to the sale of an existing asset are quite complex and the examples given here are but samples of these laws. A brief sampling of other laws is appropriate. If an asset is sold above its original cost, the difference between the sale price and the original cost is recognized as a capital gain with the difference between the original cost and the book value being recognized as ordinary income. If the company's regular income tax rate is lower than the capital gain rate, it may apply its regular income tax rate to the entire amount. If an asset is traded in instead of sold, there is no gain or loss recognized, but the beginning book value of the new asset is affected. The problem is further complicated by the fact that certain gains and losses must be set off against each other with only the net difference being recognized for taxes. In addition to these problems, the tax laws are revised frequently, making any rules of only temporary value. A detailed treatment of these problems is far beyond the scope of this book. The reader in need of detailed tax information is referred to reference items on that topic, such as the *Federal Tax Course* by Prentice-Hall.

H. IDENTIFICATION OF MARGINAL TAX FLOWS

115. When evaluating a particular capital budgeting alternative, you are interested in identifying the cash inflows and outflows that will occur *because* that alternative is chosen. Stated another way, you are interested in the *marginal cash flows* caused by the choice of a particular alternative.

113. $960
     $8,960

116. For example, suppose American Corporation is considering a new machine that will cost $30,000. It will replace an old machine that can be sold for after-tax proceeds of $10,000. The marginal cash flow to purchase the new machine is $30,000 minus the cash revenues that can be recognized from the sale of the old machine, or $_____.

117. The marginal cash inflows from an investment are also important. Assume that the old machine requires three workers at $5,000 a year, and the new machine requires only two workers at the same salary to produce the same output. The marginal labor savings from the new machine is $_____ a year.

118. In considering the effect of depreciation, we are also interested in only the marginal increase. For the above problem, assume that depreciation on the old machine was $2,000 a year and depreciation for the new machine will be $6,000 a year. Since they will sell the old machine and lose that depreciation, total depreciation will increase by only $6,000 − $2,000 = $_____.

119. You are now ready to pull the above data together to identify annual after-tax cash flows. Assume that American Corp. faces a 48% marginal tax rate.

	Income Items	Cash Flow Items
Labor Savings	$5,000	$5,000
Depreciation on New Machine $6,000		
Depreciation on Old Machine $2,000	a. _____	
Increased Profit Before Tax	b. _____	
Increased Tax	c. _____	c. _____
Increased Profit After Tax	d. ══════	
Increased Annual After-tax Cash Flows		e. ══════

Skip to Frame 123 if you got the correct answer

---

116. $20,000

117. $5,000

118. $4,000

119. (a) $4,000
     (b) 1,000
     (c)   480
     (d)   520
     (e) 4,520

120. Increased depreciation is taken directly from Frame 118.

Increased profit before tax = Labor Savings − Increased Depreciation.

Increased Tax = .48 × Increased Profit Before Tax.

Increased profit after tax = Increased profit before tax − tax.

Increased annual after tax cash flows = Labor savings − Increased tax.

This solution framework is the same as that presented in Frame 97 with the exception that depreciation is changed to show the effect of giving up depreciation from the old machine.

121. The final polishing process at ABC Corporation uses one machine with a book value of $5,000 and an estimated life of 5 years. The machine is expected to have a zero salvage value so depreciation will be $1,000 a year. They have an opportunity to replace this machine with a new machine. The new machine will cost $20,000, and they they will be able to sell the old machine for its $5,000 book value. The new machine would last five years and have a zero salvage value. Use of the new machine would reduce material expense by $5,000 a year. The company faces a 48% tax rate on regular income and a 30% tax rate on capital gains. The new machine will be depreciated to zero over a five year period if they purchase it.

The marginal cash outlay to replace the old machine with the new one will be the $20,000 cost minus the $5,000 sale of the old machine, or (a) $_____. If they kept the old machine, they would have had depreciation of $1,000. If they purchase the new machine, annual depreciation will be $4,000. Therefore, annual depreciation will increase by (b) $_____ if they replace the old machine with the new. Since material savings will be $5,000 a year and increased depreciation will be $3,000 a year, taxable income will increase by (c) $_____ a year. At the 48% marginal tax rate, taxes would increase by (d) $_____. The increase in annual after-tax cash flows would therefore be materials savings minus increased taxes or (e) $_____ .

The answer to Frame 121 appears in Frame 122.

122. The answer to the preceding problem:

Price of new machine	$20,000
Less sale of old machine	5,000
Initial cash outlay	(a) $15,000

ANNUAL CASH FLOWS:

		Income Items	Cash Flow Items
Increased profit before tax and depreciation		$5,000	$5,000
Depreciation on new machine	$4,000		
Depreciation on old machine	1,000		
Increased depreciation		(b) 3,000	
Increased profit before tax		(c) 2,000	
Increased tax		(d) 960	960
Increased profit after tax		1,040	
Increased after-tax cash flow			(e)$4,040

123. American Corporation is considering a new machine. It will cost $50,000 and will replace an existing machine which can be sold for its book value of $20,000. Either machine will last for five years and will be depreciated to zero over that period. The new machine will reduce material waste by $7,000 a year. American Corp. faces a 48% marginal tax rate. The marginal cash outlay to purchase the new machine will be $_____ and the annual after-tax cash flows will be $_____.

Skip to Frame 126 if you got the correct answer.

124. The answer to the problem in Frame 123 can be summarized as follows:

Initial cash outlay = $50,000 − $20,000 = $30,000.

		Income Items	Cash Flow Items
Increased profit before tax and depreciation		$7,000	$7,000
Depreciation on new machine	$10,000		
Depreciation on old machine	4,000		
Increased depreciation		6,000	
Increased profit before tax		1,000	
Increased tax		480	480
Increased profit after tax		$ 520	
Increased annual after-tax cash flows			$6,520

---

123. $30,000
    $6,520

125. Northwest Corporation is evaluating a new labor saving machine. The machine will cost $40,000. It will replace a machine with a book value and salvage value of $10,000. Either machine will last ten years from now and will be depreciated to zero over that time. The new machine will reduce labor expense by $7,000 a year. The company faces a 48% marginal tax rate. The initial cash outlay to replace the old machine with the new will be $_____. Depreciation will increase by $_____, and annual after-tax cash flows will increase by $_____.

H. RISK AND THE CAPITAL BUDGETING DECISION

126. As pointed out earlier, capital budgeting decisions involve the commitment of funds for long periods of time. Such decisions are normally surrounded by some degree of uncertainty concerning future events and their effect on the profitability of particular investments. Not all capital investment proposals involve the same degree of uncertainty, however. The different levels of risk should be recognized in the capital budgeting process.

127. Various methods of recognizing risk have been suggested in recent years. While there is not complete agreement on the approach to use, the general consensus is that the required rate of return, or cost of capital, increases as the risk level increases. Therefore, investments with different risk levels should be evaluated using different required rates of return. In the following chapters, the nature of risk and its effect on the cost of capital will be developed. The discussion at this time will concentrate on how the use of different required rates of return affects asset selection.

128. Great American Corporation, a widely diversified manufacturer, is evaluating competing new plant proposals from two divisions. Division A is well established in a stable market while Division B wants to move into an untried market area. Either investment will cost $20,000,000 and the company does not have sufficient funds to invest in both projects. The

---

125. $30,000
     $3,000
     $5,080

estimated net present values of the projects have been computed at three different required rates of return, as follows:

Net Present Values			
Required Rate of Return	8%	10%	12%
Project A	$10,000,000	$ 8,000,000	$7,000,000
Project B	$12,000,000	$10,000,000	$9,000,000

In the past, the company has evaluated all projects using a 10% required rate of return. If they use that approach again, project _____ will be chosen.

129. If the company decides to use different required rates of return for projects with different levels of risk, they may choose different projects. For example, if they apply a required rate of return of 12% to new ventures and 8% to divisions in stable lines of business such as A, they will choose the proposal of Division _____ .

Skip to Frame 131 if you got the correct answer.

130. At an 8% required rate of return, Division A's proposal would have a $10,000,000 net present value, while at a 12% required rate of return Division B's proposal would have a net present value of $9,000,000. They would choose in such a way as to maximize net present value so they would choose Division A's proposal.

131. Midwestern Manufacturing is considering three competing $100 million capital budgeting proposals. Project A is less risky than the company's average investment. Project B has about the same risk as the average investment for the company, and project C is somewhat more risky than average. The company has in the past applied a 10% cost of capital to all projects but is considering a move toward "risk-adjusted required rates of

---

128. B

129. A

return" by applying a 9% rate to safer than average projects and an 11% rate to riskier than average projects. The three projects have been evaluated at each of these rates of return:

NET PRESENT VALUES (000,000)			
Required Rate of Return	9%	10%	11%
Project A	$ 60	$50	$44
Project B	$ 80	$60	$50
Project C	$100	$90	$70

If they evaluate all projects at the 10% required rate of return, they will choose project _____ . If they use the proposed risk-adjusted method they will choose Project _____ .

Skip to Frame 133 if you got the correct answer.

132. If they use the risk-adjusted method, they will compare A's $60 million net present value at a 9% required rate of return with B's $60 million net present value at 10% and C's $70 million net present value at 11%. They will therefore choose Project C using risk-adjusted required rates of return.

133. As you will see later, it is rather difficult to choose the appropriate required rates of return for projects with varying degrees of risk. On the other hand, some difficult problems can arise if the company fails to recognize risk explicitly. The nature of competition is such that riskier investments typically have higher expected rates of return. Therefore, a company that evaluates projects with different risk levels at the same required rate of return may inadvertently move entirely into a much riskier group of projects. This type of error is extremely difficult to correct once it has occurred.

SUMMARY

A. PRESENT VALUE

The present value of a capital investment project is the stream of cash

---

131. C
    C

inflows from the project, *discounted* to the present using the *cost of capital.*

B. NET PRESENT VALUE

The net present value of a capital investment project is the present value of the cash inflows minus the present value of the cash outflows.

C. PROFITABILITY INDEX

The profitability index is the present value of the cash inflows divided by the present value of the cash outflows.

D. INTERNAL RATE OF RETURN

The internal rate of return is the discount or interest rate required to make the present value of the cash flows from a project equal to the cost. The internal rate of return (also referred to as the discounted rate of return) is the compound annual rate of return expected from the project.

E. PAYBACK PERIOD

The payback period is the number of years required before the sum of the cash inflows from a project equals the cost.

F. PROJECT SELECTION

The goal in capital investment selection is to *maximize net present value.* If funds are limited, they should be allocated in such a way as to maximize total net present value.

G. IDENTIFICATION OF CASH FLOWS

1. Purchase of an asset

   The purchase of a capital asset is not an expense for tax purposes. Therefore, the after-tax cash outlay equals the before-tax cost.

2. Sale of a depreciable asset

   a. Above book value but below original cost

   The difference between the sale price and the book value is taxed as ordinary income.

   b. Below book value

   The difference between the book value and the sale price is a loss and can be set against ordinary income from other sources to save taxes equal to the ordinary income tax rate times the loss on the sale.

3. Conversion from profit to cash flow

Cash flows normally equal the before-tax-and-depreciation benefits (labor savings, material savings, etc.) minus any tax on these benefits. A convenient framework for such an analysis is as follows:

	Income Items	*Cash Flow Items*
Before-tax-and-depreciation benefits	xxxxxx	xxxxxx
Increased depreciation	− xxxxxx	
Increased profit before tax	xxxxxx	
Increased tax	− xxxxxx	− xxxxxx
Increased profit after tax	xxxxxx	
Increased after-tax cash flow		xxxxxxx

H. MARGINAL ANALYSIS

It is essential that *only* the changes in cash flows caused by a particular decision be considered. In other words, we are interested only in *marginal cash flows*.

I. RISK AND THE CAPITAL BUDGETING DECISION

While there is frequent disagreement about how to treat risk, it is necessary that it be formally recognized in some way. One widely used approach is to use higher required rates of return for more risky projects. The development of appropriate required rates of return will be taken up in later chapters.

PROBLEMS

PROBLEM 1:

Midtek Corporation has a cost of capital of 10%. They are considering a new project that will cost $20,000 and will provide after-tax cash flows of $4,000 a year for ten years. Compute the present value, net present value, profitability index, internal rate of return, and payback period.

PROBLEM 2:

American Manufacturing Corporation is considering a project that costs $10,000 and provides the after-tax cash flows presented below. Using a 10% cost of capital, compute the present value, net present value, profitability index, payback period, and internal rate of return.

	After-tax Cash Flow
Year 1	$2,000
Year 2	4,000
Year 3	4,000
Year 4	6,000

PROBLEM 3:

Midwest Manufacturing Corporation has the investment opportunities shown below. They have a total of $50,000 available to invest. Which projects should they choose?

	Cost	Present Value
Project A	$10,000	$12,000
Project B	20,000	30,000
Project C	25,000	33,000
Project D	29,000	38,000
Project E	40,000	39,500

PROBLEM 4:

American Technical Corporation is subject to a 50% tax rate and a 10% cost of capital. The company is considering a new finishing machine. The machine will cost $100,000 and will reduce materials waste by an estimated $25,000 a year. The machine will last ten years and will have a zero salvage value. Straight line depreciation will be used.

a. Identify the relevant cash flows.

b. Compute the present value, net present value, and profitability index.

c. Is this an attractive project?

PROBLEM 5:

Southern Milling Corporation is considering a new automatic blender. The new blender would last for ten years and would be depreciated to zero over the ten year period. The old blender would also last for ten more years and would be depreciated to zero over the same ten year period. The old blender has a book value of $10,000 but could be sold for $15,000 (the original cost was $20,000). The new blender would cost $50,000. It would reduce labor expense by $6,000 a year. The company is subject to a 50% tax rate on regular income and a 30% tax rate on capital gains. Their cost of capital is 8%.

a. Identify all the relevant cash flows for this replacement decision.

b. Compute the present value, net present value, and profitability index.

c. Is this an attractive project?

SOLUTIONS

SOLUTION 1:

Present value = $4,000 × 6.145 = $24,580

Net present value = $24,580 − $20,000 = $4,580

Profitability index = $24,580/$20,000 = 1.229

Internal rate of return:

The internal rate of return is found by a trial and error process of solving for the present value at various discount rates until we find the rate that gives a present value closest to the cost. For this project, the present values are computed at various interest rates as shown below.

Interest Rate	Present value computation
10%	$4,000 × 6.145 = $24,580
12%	$4,000 × 5.650 = $22,600
14%	$4,000 × 5.216 = $20,864
16%	$4,000 × 4.833 = $19,332

Since the present value would equal the cost ($20,000) at some interest rate between 14% and 16%, the internal rate of return is between 14% and 16%.

Payback Period: At $4,000 cash flow per year, they will have recovered the cost by the end of 5 years.

SOLUTION 2:

	Cash Flow	Present Value Factor	Present Value
Year 1	$2,000	.909	$1,818
Year 2	4,000	.826	3,304
Year 3	4,000	.751	3,004
Year 4	6,000	.683	4,098
			Total = $12,224

Present value = $12,224
Net present value = $12,224 − $10,000 = $2,224
Profitability index = $12,224/$10,000 = 1.2224
Payback period = 3 years
Internal rate of return:
The internal rate of return is found by a trial and error process of solving for the present value at various discount rates until we find the rate that gives a present value closest to the cost. For this project, the present values are computed at various interest rates as follows:

	Cash Flow	Present Value Factor (16%)	Present Value
Year 1	$2,000	.862	$1,724
Year 2	4,000	.743	2,972
Year 3	4,000	.641	2,564
Year 4	6,000	.552	3,312
			Total = $10,572

At a discount rate of 16% the present value is still above the cost. Therefore, the internal rate of return is over 16%.

SOLUTION 3:

You should choose projects in such a way as to maximize net present value subject to the limit of $50,000 available to invest. The net present values of the individual projects are as follows:

	Cost	Present Value	Net Present Value
Project A	$10,000	$12,000	$ 2,000
Project B	20,000	30,000	10,000
Project C	25,000	33,000	8,000
Project D	29,000	38,000	9,000
Project E	40,000	39,500	− 500

Project E can be eliminated immediately since it has a negative net present value. Of the combinations possible within the $50,000 constraint, projects *B and D* are best. The selection of this combination will provide a total net present value of $10,000 + $9,000 = $19,000.

SOLUTION 4:

a. The cash outlay to purchase the new machine will be $100,000. Annual depreciation will be $100,000/10 = $10,000. Annual cash flows can be identified as follows:

Annual Material Savings	$25,000	$25,000
Increased Depreciation	10,000	
Increased Profit Before Tax	15,000	
Increased Tax	7,500	7,500
Increased Profit After Tax	7,500	
Increased Annual After-Tax Cash Flows		$17,500

b.

Years	Cash Flow	Present Value Factor	Present Value
1 - 10	$17,500	6.145	$107,538

Present Value = $107,538
Net Present Value = $107,538 − $100,000 = $7,538
Profitability Index = $107,538/$100,000 = 1.075

c. This is an attractive project. It has a net present value greater than zero.

SOLUTION 5:

a. Tax on the sale of the old machine:

Original cost	$20,000	
Sale price	15,000	$5,000 × .50 = $2,500 Tax on sale
Book value	10,000	

After-tax cash receipts from sale of old machine:

Sale price	$15,000
Taxes on sale	2,500
After-tax cash receipts	$12,500

Net cash flow to replace old machine with new:

Cost of the new machine	$50,000
After-tax receipt from sale of old machine	12,500
Net cash flow to replace old machine with new	$37,500

Depreciation on new machine = $50,000/10 = $5,000
Depreciation on old machine = $10,000/10 = $1,000

		Income Items	Cash Flow Items
Annual Labor Savings		$6,000	$6,000
Depreciation on New Machine	$5,000		
Depreciation on Old Machine	1,000		
Increased Depreciation		4,000	
Increased Earnings Before Tax		2,000	
Increased Tax		1,000	1,000
Increased Earnings After Tax		$1,000	
Increased After-tax Cash Flow			$5,000

b.

	Cash Flow	Present Value Factor	Present Value
1 - 10	$5,000	6.710	$33,550

Net Present Value − $33,550 − $37,500 = −$3,950
Profitability Index = $33,550/$37,500 = .895

c. This is *not* an attractive project.

7

VALUE

The topic of value is central to finance. During the study of value, the similarity between valuation and present value techniques of capital budgeting will be noted. This is because capital budgeting techniques are an application of value theory. When moving on from value to cost of capital estimation, it will be noted that cost of capital estimation is another application of value theory. In addition, an understanding of value is extremely helpful for topics such as security analysis and merger evaluation.

According to economists, a thing must be scarce and provide utility in order to be valuable. Air is useful but not scarce. Therefore, it has no value fron an economic viewpoint; nobody will buy air. This chapter is primarily concerned with the value of capital assets. Examples of such assets are a machine, a factory, a bond, or a share of stock. Capital assets have value because they generate earnings. A bond is valuable because it pays a stream of interest payments plus the eventual repayment of the principal. A machine is valuable because it produces a product which can be sold to create income. A company is valuable to its shareholders because it creates income and pays a stream of dividends to its shareholders. It should be noted that in each case the earnings we are primarily interested in are in the form of a cash flow to the owners as opposed to accounting income. It is this cash flow which can be used to acquire additional goods and which ultimately gives the asset value. Capital assets are scarce and provide utility in the form of a stream of earnings, or cash flows.

In this chapter the principles of capital asset valuation are developed. On completing this chapter, you will understand and be able to apply the fundamental principles of capital asset valuation to specific assets or total companies.

A. VALUE CONCEPTS

1. For a thing to have value, it must be _____ and provide _____. Air is not valuable because it is not _____.

2. Capital assets have value because they are able to generate _____.

B. BOND VALUE

3. Since the value of a capital asset is derived from the stream of earnings (cash flows) it can generate, the techniques of present value analysis apply here. The value of a bond provides a good illustration of this. The value of a bond equals the present value of all the future cash flows associated with it. For a bond, these cash flows consist of the interest payments on the bond and the principal repayment at the time of its retirement.

4. A particular bond has a face value of $1,000 and pays interest of 10% or $100 a year. The bond will be retired at the end of ten years. For simplicity it is assumed that the interest on the bond is paid at the end of each year for the next ten years. The cash flows, therefore, consist of $_____ at the end of each year for the next ten years plus an additional $1,000 at the end of ten years. If an investor required an 8% return on his investment, he would use the present value method to compute the value of the bond as follows:

Year	Cash Flow	Present Value Factor	Present Value
1-10	$100	6.710	$671.00
10	$1,000	.463	463.00
			$1,134.00

Therefore, if the required rate of return is 8%, the value of the bond is $_____.

---

1. scarce   4. $100
   utility $1,134.00
   scarce

2. earnings or cash flows

5. If the required rate of return was 12%, the value of the bond would be
_____ .

Skip to Frame 8 if you got the correct answer.

6. The answer to Frame 5 is computed as follows:

Year	Cash Flow	Present Value Factor	Present Value
1-10	$ 100	5.650*	$565
10	$1,000	.322**	322
			$887

*From Table IV
**From Table II

If you had trouble with the identification of cash flows, refer back to
Frame 4. The cash flows are the same. If you had difficulty in locating the
correct present value factors in the tables, review Chapter 5 on present
value before continuing.

7. If the required rate of return was 14%, the value of the bond would be
$_____ .

8. If the required rate of return was 10%, the value of the bond would be
$_____ .

9. You will note that as the *required rate of return* goes up, the value of the
bond goes *up / down.*

10. There are two factors affecting the value of a bond. One is the expected
stream of cash flows, and the other is the _____
_____ _____ _____ .

---

5. $887.00

7. $100×5.216 + $1,000×.270 = *$791.60*

8. $1,000 or $1,000.50 (The difference caused by rounding in the tables.)

9. down

10. required rate of return

C. PREFERRED STOCK VALUATION

11. Like a bond, a stock's value is determined by the expected cash flows and the _____ .

12. A preferred stock has no maturity and normally pays a fixed dividend. Therefore, the value of a preferred stock equals the present value of a perpetual stream of dividends, or

$$V = D/Kp$$

where:

   V = Value
   D = Annual dividend
   Kp = Required rate of return

13. A certain preferred stock pays dividends of $4 per year. The required rate of return is 8%. The value of the stock, therefore, is

   $$V = \$4/.08 = \ \$\underline{\hspace{2in}}$$

14. If the required rate of return increased to 10%, the value of the stock would decline to $_____ .

Skip to Frame 16 if you got the correct answer.

15. If the required rate of return declines to 5%, the value of the stock will increase to $_____ .

16. Like the bond, the value of the preferred stock is determined by the expected _____ and the _____

   _____ .

---

   11. required rate of return

   13. $50

   14. $4/.10 = *$40*

   15. $4/.05 = *$80*

   16. cash flows
       required rate of return

C. COMMON STOCK VALUATION

17. The same general principles apply to a share of common stock. Its value is also determined by the expected cash flows (dividends) and the required rate of return. Unfortunately, the valuation of common stock is complicated by several factors. First, common stocks seldom pay the same dividend for an infinite time period. The dividends change as the fortunes of the company change. Further, the stockholder may receive another kind of cash flow. He may expect to sell the stock at some future date and receive cash from the sale. Each of these complications will be dealt with in the following frames.

18. The solution to these problems is another application of present value analysis. As an example, suppose you had a common stock that had a life of only three years. The stock was expected to pay dividends of $10 in the first year, $20 in the second year, and $30 in the third year. For simplicity, assume that each year's dividends are received at the end of the year. At the end of three years the company will cease to operate and the stock will be worthless. If an investor's required rate of return is 10%, the determination of the value of the stock is a simple problem of present value analysis, as follows:

Year	Cash Flow	Present Value Factor*	Present Value
1	$10	.909	$ 9.09
2	20	.826	16.52
3	30	.751	22.53
			$48.14

*From Table II

19. For the stock discussed in Frame 18, if the investor required a 12% rate of return, the value of the stock would be _____ .

---

19. Year	Cash Flow	PV Factor	Present Value
1	$10	.893	$ 8.93
2	20	.797	15.94
3	30	.712	21.36
			$46.23

Review Chapter 5 if you missed this problem for reasons other than a careless error.

20. You will note that as the required rate of return increases, the value of a particular stream of dividends *increases / decreases* .

21. The basic principles underlying the valuation of common stock have now been established. The value of the share of stock is the *present value of all future dividends* . While the above problems illustrated the finding of value with only three years of dividends expected, it is obviously possible to extend this analysis to any number of years. The concept is the same, but the computations become tedious.

22. As another example, an investor wishes to earn an 8% return on his money. He intends to invest in the stock of a company that will automatically liquidate at the end of three years. The company will be worth nothing at the end of the three years. The dividends expected over the three years are shown below. Find the value of the stock to the investor.

Year	Dividends
1	$30
2	$20
3	$20

Skip to Frame 25 if you got the correct answer.

23. The answer to Frame 22 appears as follows:

Year	Dividends	P.V. Factor*	Present Value
1	$30	.926	$27.78
2	20	.857	17.14
3	20	.794	15.88
			$60.80

*From Table II.

---

20. decreases

22. $60.80

24. If the investor required a 10% rate of return, the value of the stock would be $_____.

25. We have now evaluated the theoretical method of evaluating a share of common stock. Unfortunately, while the concept does not change, the calculations would become extremely tedious because most companies are expected to continue in operation indefinitely. Further, the dividends expected in the distant future are extremely difficult to estimate. One might, therefore, ask why time is being spent on this type of calculation. The answer is that the purpose of this discussion is to give an understanding of the factors which affect the value of a share of common stock. This understanding is critical to the study of much of finance.

26. In the previous problems, it was assumed that the investor intended to hold the common stock for its entire life. If the investor intends to sell the stock at some future time, how does this affect his estimation of its value? Once, again, the simple stock used in the example of Frame 18 will be used. The present value of all future dividends for that stock, discounted at 10%, was $ _____. Suppose, however, the investor only expects to hold the stock for one year and sell it. If he sells it one year from now, he is selling the remainder of the dividend stream, or a payment of $20 one year away and a payment of $30 two years away. Therefore, at the end of one year the value of the stock will be:

$20 × .909 + $30 × .826 = $ _____.

Thus, the investor who buys the stock today expects to receive at the end of one year a $10 dividend plus the $42.96 sale price, or a total of $_____. The present value of $52.96 received one year from today, at a required rate of return of 10% is .909 × $52.96 = $_____. You will note that this $48.14 is the same value you computed under the assumption that the investor intended to hold the stock for its entire life.

---

24. Year	Dividends	P.V. Factor	Present Value	**26.** $48.14
1	$30	.909	$27.27	$42.96
2	$20	.826	16.52	$52.96
3	$20	.751	15.02	$48.14
			$58.81	

27. Suppose you buy the above stock with the intention of selling it two years from now. The value two years from now is the present value of $30 received in one year or .909 X $30 = $_____. The value of the stock today equals the present value of the next two years' dividends plus the present value of the $27.27 sale price. The value of the stock, therefore, is $_____.

Skip to Frame 30 if you got the correct answer.

28. The answer to Frame 27 is as follows:

Item	Year	Cash Flow	P.V. Factor	Present Value
Dividend	1	$10	.909	$ 9.09
Dividend	2	20	.826	16.52
Sale Price	2	27.27	.826	22.53
				$48.14

You will again note that the value of the stock depends on the expected stream of dividends, and not on when you intend to sell it.

29. Refer to Frame 22. The value of the stock examined in that frame was $ _____. If the investor expects to sell the stock after one year, the value of the stock today is the present value of the first year's dividend plus the present value of the sale price, or a total value of $ _____. Plans to sell the stock in the future *do / do not* affect its value.

30. It was said earlier that the value of a capital asset is the present value of the cash flows it can generate, discounted at the required rate of return. It has been shown that the same valuation procedure applies to bonds, preferred stock, and common stock. It was, however, also pointed out that the valuation of common stock is a very complex problem in actual practice.

---

27. $27.27   29. $60.80
    $48.14 $20 X .926 + $20 X .857 = $35.66;
                         ($35.66 + $30) X .926 = *$60.80*

31. There are some special cases where simplified models can be used to determine the value of a share of common stock. One is the case where dividends are expected to remain constant indefinitely. In this case, the value of a share of common stock is computed in the same manner as a share of preferred stock. Southern Electric's common stock pays an annual dividend of $4. This level of dividend payment is expected to continue indefinitely. At a required rate of return of 8%, the value of Southern's common stock is $4/.08 = $_____.

32. At a 10% required rate of return, the value of a share of Southern's common stock is $ _____.

33. Another special case is the situation where dividends are expected to grow at a constant rate forever. In this case, the value of a share of common stock is:

$$V = \frac{D}{Ke - g} *$$

where:

D = Present annual dividend
Ke = Required rate of return
g = Annual percentage growth in dividends expected

*The proof of this is available in most advanced finance texts.

34. ABM currently pays dividends of $5 a year. Dividends are expected to increase at a rate of 5% a year. The required rate of return is 10%. The value of a share of ABM stock is:

$$V = \frac{5}{.10 - .05} = \$\underline{\hspace{2cm}}$$

35. American Corporation pays dividends of $4 a year. The dividends are expected to grow at 6% a year and the required rate of return is 10%. The value of a share of American Corporation common stock is $_____.

---

31. $50

32. $4/.10 = *$40*

34. $5/.05 = *$100*

35. $4/(.10−.06) = *$100*

Skip to Frame 37 if you got the correct answer.

36. If the expected growth rate for American Corporation's dividends changes from 6% to 5% and other factors remain unchanged, the value of American Corporation's common stock will change to $_____ .

37. To develop a further understanding of value, it will be helpful to look at the effect of an expected change in the interest rate on value. The stock introduced in Frame 18 will be used again. The value of the stock was $_____ when evaluated at a 10% required rate of return. In Frame 26, it was shown that the intention to sell the stock at some future date instead of holding it for its entire life *did / did not* change the value. In Frame 19, however, it was shown that a change in the required rate of return would change the value.

38. Another problem is now introduced. Suppose the required rate of return is now 10% but is expected to rise to 12% at the end of the first year and the investor expects to sell the stock at that time. Therefore, the value of the stock one year from now will be the present value of the remaining dividends, discounted at 12%, or $_____ . The total cash flow received by today's purchaser will be the dividend of $10 at the end of one year plus the $41.77 sale price in one year, or a total of $_____ received at the end of one year. The value of the stock equals the present value of $51.77 received one year from now, discounted at 10%, or $_____ .

39. For the same stock, suppose the required rate of return is expected to fall to 8% at the end of the first year. If all other factors are the same as in Frame 38, the value of the stock today will be $_____ .

Skip to Frame 42 if you got the correct answer.

---

36. $4 / (.10 − .05) = *$80*

37. $48.14
    did not

38. $20 × .893 + $30 × .797 = *$41.77*
    $51.77
    $51.77 × .909 = *$47.06*

39. $49.30

40. The answer to the preceding problem:

The anticipated value at the end of the first year is:

$.926 \times \$20 + .857 \times \$30 = \$44.23$

Total cash flow anticipated is the $10 dividend at the end of the first year plus the $44.23 sale price at the end of the first year, for a total of *$54.23*.

The value of the stock equals the present value of $54.23 received one year from now, discounted at 10%, or $54.23 $\times$ .909 = $49.30.

41. For the problem described in Frame 39, if the interest rate is expected to fall to 6% instead of 8% at the end of the first year, the value of the stock today is $_____ .

42. You will note that while plans to sell the stock at some future date did not change its value, an anticipated change in the required rate of return did change it. This simple stock is, of course, unrealistic in that its life ends in three years. Most stocks will have extremely long expected lives and the effect of an expected future change in interest rates will be even greater than for this simple example.

43. As mentioned earlier, it is extremely difficult to determine the dividends expected over an extremely long time period. For this reason, analysts frequently look at the earnings per share (net income divided by number of shares of common stock outstanding) of the company as well as the cash flow in the form of dividends. One argument for doing this is that the earnings represent a gain to the shareholders. The difference between the earnings and dividends represents an amount that was reinvested to provide future returns for the shareholders. When this approach is used, an "earnings multiple" or price-earnings ratio is assigned by some method such as looking at the earnings multiples of other companies. The earnings multiple, or price-earnings ratio, is merely the price of a share of stock divided by the earnings per share. By determining the average price-earnings ratio for the same or similar industries, a guideline is developed for valuing a particular company's earnings. The multiple is then adjusted upward or downward based on whether the analyst feels the outlook for the company is better or worse than for its industry.

---

41. $20 $\times$ .943 + $30 $\times$ .890 = $45.56;
($45.56 + $10) $\times$ .909 = *$50.50*

44. AFM Corporation's common stock is selling at $40 a share and earnings per share are $4.00. AFM's price-earnings ratio is 40/4 = _____. The average price-earnings ratio for the industry is 12. If the price-earnings ratio for AFM were 12, its price would be $_____. If the outlook for AFM is considered by the investor to be as good or better than the rest of the industry, it would appear that it is *underpriced / overpriced*. If it is underpriced, you could say that its value exceeds its price. The stock would therefore be considered an attractive buy relative to other companies in the industry.

45. Amtel Corporation's common stock is currently selling for $50 a share and its earnings are $5 a share. The average price-earnings ratio for the industry is 9 and you feel that the outlook for Amtel is not as good as that for the rest of the industry. According to your analysis, Amtel's common stock is *underpriced / overpriced*. By your estimate, the value of Amtel common stock is *greater / less* than the market price.

Skip to Frame 48 if you got the correct answer.

46. If you felt that the outlook for Amtel was about the same as that for the industry, a price earnings ratio of 9 and therefore a price of 9 × $5 = $45 would be appropriate relative to the rest of the industry. Since you estimate the outlook for Amtel to be poorer than that for the rest of the industry, a price of less than $45 or a price-earnings ratio of less than 9 would be appropriate. Therefore, it would be your feeling that the value is *greater / less* than the price.

47. If the price-earnings ratio for the industry were 11 and you felt that the outlook for Amtel was better than that for the industry in general, then you would feel that the stock was *overpriced / underpriced* at $50, or that the value was *greater / less* than the price.

---

44. 10
$4 × 12 = $48
underpriced

45. overpriced
less

46. less

47. underpriced
greater

48. One other approach to determining the value of a share of common stock or a company will be presented here. This method requires little or no calculation. You can merely accept the market's estimate of value, or the price of the stock. This approach is not entirely without merit. The price of a share of stock represents the consensus of investors relative to its value. When evaluating companies for a potential merger, the company being acquired would have a difficult time explaining any price below the current market price to their shareholders. Using this approach, if the price of a share of American Corp. common stock is $70, you therefore assume that the value is $_____ .

D. VALUATION OF A COMPANY

49. The next step in the analysis is to apply what has been learned to the valuation of a company. The principle is exactly the same as for individual securities. A business enterprise has value because it can generate a stream of cash flows for its owners. The total value of the company is the value of its equity plus the value of the creditor claims. The value of the equity of a corporation is merely the value of a share of its common stock times the number of shares outstanding.

50. FCM Corporation has current liabilities of $100,000, long term debt worth $100,000, and 10,000 shares of common stock worth $10 each. The total value of the shareholders' claim is $_____ and the total value of FCM Corporation is $_____ .

Skip to Frame 52 if you got the correct answer.

51. If the value of a share of FCM common stock increases to $20 and all other factors remain unchanged, the total value of the shareholders' claim will be $_____ and the total value of FCM Corporation will be $_____ .

---

48. $70

50. $100,000
$300,000

51. $200,000
$400,000

E. DETERMINATION OF THE REQUIRED RATE OF RETURN

52. The required rate of return has been central to much of the analysis in this chapter. Up to this point, it has merely been assumed that the required rate of return is known. In this section, the major factors affecting the required rate of return are considered. The required rate of return is determined by two major factors: the general level of interest rates and the perceived risk associated with a particular investment. The general level of interest rates reflects the returns available to investors from alternate investments. The yield on U.S. Government securities reflects the returns available on risk-free investments. This information is available monthly in the *Federal Reserve Bulletin* as well as other sources.

53. This section concentrates on how risk affects the required rate of return. In general, it can be said that the greater the level of risk, the greater the required rate of return. But this section is specific about that relationship.

54. Risk can be divided into two main categories, systematic and unsystematic. *Unsystematic risk* has to do with characteristics unique to a particular investment. For example, consider a new product which a company is going to introduce. Consumers may reject the product because it does not suit their tastes or because competing products meet their needs better. This risk of failure is unique to the particular project and is not related to overall market conditions. It is, therefore, referred to as unsystematic risk. If you decide to drill an oil well, the risk of not hitting oil is not related to overall market conditions and is therefore an example of *systematic / unsystematic* risk.

55. *Systematic risk*, on the other hand, is related to overall market conditions. A product may meet the needs of the public better than all competing products and still be a failure. The product could fail because general economic conditions decline and the public cannot afford it. The product discussed in Frame 54 may fail because a depression drives overall demand downward. This type of risk is called systematic risk because it is related to the general economic system. You decide to build a steel plant. The risk of overall steel demand being driven down by a recession is an example of *systematic / unsystematic* risk.

---

54. unsystematic

55. systematic

56. Investors can eliminate the effects of unsystematic risk through diversification. For example, by purchasing stock in all automobile manufacturers, it is possible to "average out" the auto companies with below average profits and sales against those with above average returns. Therefore, unsystematic risk is also referred to as *diversifiable risk*. Since investors can eliminate the effects of unsystematic risk through diversification, it should cause them little anguish. Therefore, the required rate of return should not be greatly affected by unsystematic risk. Systematic risk, on the other hand, is nondiversifiable and cannot be eliminated by combining with other investments. Spreading your investment across all the auto companies will not protect you from the fact that the sales of all auto companies tend to decline in a recession. A very large and well diversified portfolio will still tend to go up in value when general market conditions improve and go down when general market conditions decline. It is this systematic or nondiversifiable portion of risk for which the investor must be compensated. *The required rate of return will be a function of the general level of interest rates and the systematic risk associated with a particular investment.*

57. To summarize, then, unsystematic risk is *diversifiable / nondiversifiable*. It is related to factors unique to a particular investment. Since its effect can be eliminated through diversification, the required rate of return is not heavily affected by unsystematic risk. Systematic risk, on the other hand, is *diversifiable / nondiversifiable*. It is related to the effects of general economic conditions. Since it cannot be diversified away, there must be some incentive for accepting risk. The incentive is in the form of a higher required rate of return. The required rate of return, therefore, is a function of the general level of interest rates and _____ risk.

58. Several methods of measuring systematic risk have been suggested. The most widely used of these is *beta*. Beta is a measure of the sensitivity of returns for a particular investment to returns for the market in general. The beta can best be shown using a graph. It is illustrated for the common stock of a particular company. Over a period of time, you observe that when the stock market in general rises, the price of this particular stock tends to rise, and when the stock market in general declines, the price of

---

57. diversifiable
    nondiversifiable
    systematic or nondiversifiable

this particular stock also tends to fall. You have observed the returns (dividends and price appreciation) a holder of this security would have received during each of a number of years and observed the return that an investor would have received during each of these periods if he had held some broad-based portfolio, represented by the Dow-Jones industrial average, or some other index. Each dot on the following graph represents one of your observations. The line is drawn to fit the dots as closely as possible. The line, then, represents the return you might expect from the security at any given level of return for the market. For example, using this line, if return for the market index were 8% for a particular year, you would expect return on the security to be _____%. If return for the market were 0%, you would expect return for the security to be _____%.

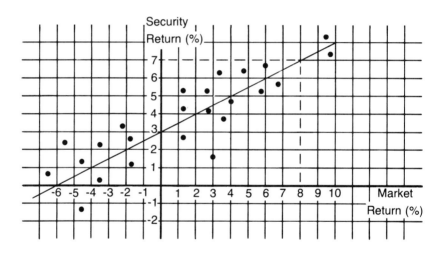

You will note, therefore, that as the market return goes from 0% to 8%, expected return on the security goes from 3% to 7%, or a change of 4%. Expected return for the security changes by 1/2 as much as return for the market. Therefore, the security has a beta of 0.5.

---

58. 7%
    3%

59. A 4% loss for the market would be expected to result in a _____ %
    gain / loss for the security.

60. Beta, then, is a measure of systematic or nondiversifiable risk. The beta for
    a security is the expected percentage point change in return for each
    percentage point change in return for the stock market average.

61. As an example, suppose average return for the market is expected
    to be 8% and expected return for a particular security is 10%. Conditions
    that would cause market return to increase to 9% would be expected to
    cause return for the security to increase to 12%. The beta for the security,
    then, would be:

$$b = \frac{.12 - .10}{.09 - .08} = \underline{}$$

62. Obviously, for any particular security during any particular year, the above
    relationship will not hold precisely. If return for the market reaches 9%
    during a particular year, return for the security may be above or below
    12%, depending on factors affecting that particular security. For example,
    return to investors holding the stock of a particular company will depend
    on consumer acceptance of that company's products as well as overall
    market conditions. Once again, a well diversified portfolio can cancel out
    the risk associated only with that particular security. The expected
    relationship between the security and the market cannot be cancelled out
    by diversification.

63. The required rate of return is a function of the rate of return on risk free
    investments, such as long term government bonds, and the systematic risk,
    represented by beta. A major body of finance literature suggests that the
    required rate of return may be stated as follows:

$$Ke = R + b(Em - R)$$

where:

$$Ke = \text{required rate of return}$$
$$R = \text{risk-free interest rate}$$
$$b = \text{beta}$$
$$Em = \text{expected average return for common stocks in general}$$

---

59. 1%
      gain

61. 2

The term (Em − R) is the difference between expected return for the stock market average and the risk-free interest rate. It is the average compensation for risk in the securities market, or the risk premium. The risk premium for a particular security is obtained by multiplying the average risk premium by the security's beta. The risk premium for a particular stock, therefore, is a function of its beta and the risk premium for the market in general. Betas for many companies are computed and published by investment services such as *Value Line*.

64. As an example, suppose that expected return for the stock market in general is 9% per year and that the yield on long-term U.S. government bonds is 6%. Plain States Power Company is relatively stable, with a beta of 0.5. The required return for Plain States common stock is estimated to be:

$$Ke = .06 + .5(.09 - .06) = .06 + .015 = \text{_____}$$

65. Assume that general market conditions are the same as those described in Frame 64. LMN Corporation has a beta of 2. The required return for LMN common stock is _____.

Skip to Frame 67 if you got the correct answer.

66. If the beta for LMN had been 1, the required rate of return would have been _____ .

67. MIS Corporation is not publicly traded so no market price for its shares is available. Dividends are currently $4.20 per share with no growth anticipated. Earnings per share are $5.00. The average price-earnings ratio for publicly traded companies in the industry is 13. Expected return for the market as a whole is 9% and the yield on long term government securities is 6%. The average beta for companies in the industry is .333. Using the earnings multiple approach, the value of a share of MIS stock is estimated to be $_____ . The required rate of return is estimated at _____ %. Using the dividend capitalization approach, the value of a share of stock is estimated at $_____ .

---

64. .075 or 7.5%

65. .06 + 2(.09 − .06) = .06 + .06 = *.12*

66. .09 or 9%

67. $65
.07
$60

Skip to Frame 70 if you got the correct answer.

68. The answers to Frame 67 are computed as follows:

    Earnings multiple approach: V = 13 X $5 = *$65*

    Required rate of return: Ke = .06 + .333(.09 − .06) = *.07*

    Dividend capitalization approach: V = $4.20/.07 = *$60*

    Refer back to Frames 43 to 47 for a review of the earnings multiple approach. Refer back to Frames 31 and 32 for a review of the dividend capitalization approach.

69. General stock prices have declined to the point where the average price-earnings ratio for the industry is 11 and the expected return for the market as a whole is 10%. Also, the yield on long-term U.S. government securities has increased to 7%. The dividends and earnings per share of MIS have not changed. Rework the answers to Frame 67 based on these assumptions.

70. Using the figures given in Frame 67 (ignore the modifications in Frame 69), but assuming that dividends for MIS are expected to grow at 1% per year, recompute the answers to Frame 67.

    Skip to the summary if you got the correct answer.
    Refer to Frames 33 to 36 if you did not remember how to use the dividend growth rate in computing value.

71. If the expected dividend growth rate for MIS is expected to be 2% per year, the value would be computed at $_____ per share using the dividend capitalization approach.

---

69. V = $5 X 11 = *$55*
    Ke = .07 + .333(.10 − .07) = *.08*
    V = $4.20/.08 = $52.50

70. V = $5 X 13 = *$65*
    Ke = .06 + 333(.09 − .06) = *.07*
    V = $4.20/(.07 − .01) = *$70*

71. V = $4.20/ (.07 − .02) = *$84*

SUMMARY

A. BASIS OF VALUE

1. To have value, a thing must be *scarce* and provide *utility*.
2. Capital assets have value because they are able to generate earnings or *cash flows*.

B. BOND VALUE

1. The value of a bond equals the present value of the stream of interest payments plus the present value of the repayment, all discounted at the required rate of return.
2. For example, a $1,000 bond pays interest of $100 at the end of each year and is 10 years from maturity. At an 8% required rate of return, the value of the bond is:

$$V = \$100 \times 6.710 + \$1,000 \times .463 = \$1,134$$

C. PREFERRED STOCK VALUE

1. A share of preferred stock normally pays a constant dividend indefinitely. The value, therefore, is an infinite stream of dividends discounted at the required rate of return.
2. For example, if the required rate of return is 10%, the value of a share of stock paying dividends of $5 a year is:

$$V = D/K_p = 5/.10 = \$50$$

D. COMMON STOCK VALUE

1. The value of a common stock is also the present value of all future dividends, discounted at the required rate of return. Direct evaluation of the expected future stream of dividends is called the *dividend capitalization* approach to stock value.

   a. If the dividends are expected to remain constant indefinitely, the valuation process is the same as that for preferred stock.

   $$V = D/K_e$$

   where:
   D = Annual dividend payment
   K_e = Required rate of return

   b. If dividends are expected to grow at a constant rate indefinitely, the value of a share of stock is:

$$V = D/(Ke - g)$$

where:

g = Expected annual growth in dividends

2. Since it is difficult to forecast dividends at distant future dates, other means of common stock valuation are sometimes used. One of these is the earnings multiple approach. Under this method, the earnings per share of the company are multiplied by an earnings multiple or price earnings ratio to arrive at an estimate of value. The appropriate price-earnings ratio is determined by such methods as looking at the price-earnings ratios of similar companies or industries.

3. A final approach to value is to merely accept the present market price of the stock as its value. This price does, after all, represent some kind of consensus as to the value of the stock.

E. THE REQUIRED RATE OF RETURN

1. The required rate of return is the return investors must expect if they are to be induced to invest in a specific asset.

2. The required rate of return equals the risk-free interest rate plus a risk premium, or additional expected return to compensate investors for accepting risk.

3. Risk can be divided into systemic and unsystematic risk.

   a. Unsystematic risk is unique to a particular investment. Its effects can be neutralized through diversification.

   b. Systematic risk is related to general market conditions and is not diversifiable. It is this risk for which the investor must be compensated.

4. Systematic risk can be measured in terms of the security's beta. The beta measures the sensitivity of return for the particular security to general market conditions.

5. The higher the beta, the greater is the required rate of return. This may be stated as follows:

$$Ke = R + b(Em - R)$$

where:

R = Risk-free interest rate

b = Beta

Em = Expected average return for the market as a whole

PROBLEMS

PROBLEM 1:

A $1,000 bond has 20 years remaining until maturity. It pays interest of 10% of the face value of the bond or $100 at the end of each year. An investor who required a 12% return on his investment would be willing to pay a maximum of $_____ for the bond.

PROBLEM 2:

A share of preferred stock pays dividends of $8 a year. An investor who required a 10% return on his investment would be willing to pay a maximum of $_____ for a share of the preferred stock.

PROBLEM 3:

A hypothetical company has a life of only 5 years, at the end of which time it will be worthless. The expected dividends are shown below. Find the value of the stock at a 10% required rate of return.

	Expected Dividend
Year 1	$10
Year 2	10
Year 3	10
Year 4	20
Year 5	30

PROBLEM 4:

American Corporation is expected to pay a constant dividend of $8 a year indefinitely. The value of a share of its stock, at a 10% required rate of return is $_____ .

PROBLEM 5:

If dividends for the above company were expected to grow indefinitely at 2% a year, the value of a share of stock would be $_____ .

PROBLEM 6:

Earnings per share for Amacom Corporation are $12 and the average price earnings ratio for Amacom's industry is 8. Estimate the value of a share of Amacom stock using the earnings multiple approach.

PROBLEM 7:

Express Corporation has $1,000,000 of current liabilities. The company has outstanding a bond issue with a book value of $2,000,000. The bonds pay interest of $200,000 at the end of each year and have 10 years until maturity. The general level of interest rates has declined to 8% for bonds of similar companies and the current market value of Express Corporation's bonds totals $2,268,000. The company has 100,000 shares of common stock outstanding. The total book value of the owners' equity is $2,000,000. Earnings per share are $3 and while Express's common stock is not actively traded, the average price earnings ratio for the industry is 10. Estimate the value of a share of Express Corporation common stock, the total value of the shareholders' equity, and the total value of Express Corporation to all investors and creditors.

SOLUTIONS

SOLUTION 1:

	Cash Flow	Present Value Factor	Present Value
Years 1-20	$ 100	7.469	$746.90
Year 20	1,000	.104	104.00
		Maximum Value =	$850.90

SOLUTION 2:

V = $8/.10 = $80

SOLUTION 3:

	Expected Dividend	Present Value Factor	Present Value
Year 1	$10	.909	$ 9.09
Year 2	10	.826	8.26
Year 3	10	.751	7.51
Year 4	20	.683	13.66
Year 5	30	.621	18.63
			$57.15

SOLUTION 4:

$V = \$8 / .10 = \underline{\$80}$

SOLUTION 5:

$V = \$8/(.10 - .02) = \underline{\$100}$

SOLUTION 6:

$V = \$12 \times 8 = \underline{\$96}$

SOLUTION 7:

Estimated value per share = $\$3 \times 10 = \$30$

Estimated total value of shareholders' equity = $\$30 \times 100,000 = \$3,000,000$

Estimated Total value to all investors and creditors:

Current Liabilities (value to current creditors)	$1,000,000
Long Term Debt (total market value)	2,268,000
Common Stock (estimated total value)	3,000,000
	$6,268,000

8

COST OF CAPITAL

The cost of capital is the cost of funds to the firm. This is usually thought of as the *opportunity cost*, or the return investors could expect from an alternative opportunity of equal risk. If a company is to successfully compete for funds, it must be able to earn returns that are at least equal to the returns available from the other opportunities available to investors.

The most important use of the cost of capital is in the capital budgeting process. In order to evaluate capital investments, it is necessary to have an accurate estimate of the cost of funds that will be invested. The quality of the final capital budgeting decision will depend on the quality of the original cost of capital estimates. In addition, certain other areas of finance, such as inventory and accounts receivable policy include the cost of funds tied up as one of the costs. These decisions therefore rely on the cost of capital estimates.

The term *capital structure* refers to the mix of long term funds used by the firm. The primary components are long term debt of various types, preferred stock, and common stock. The typical firm will use some combination of these sources in an effort to achieve a minimum cost of capital.

Several important factors affect the firm's cost of capital. As mentioned previously, the cost of capital is an opportunity cost, or the return investors could expect from alternative opportunities of equal risk. One factor in the cost of capital is the general level of investment opportunities available. The general level of opportunities is reflected in the overall level of interest rates in the market. Also, investors must expect a higher rate of return if they are to be pursuaded to invest in more risky assets. The more risk connected with the asset structure of the firm, the higher will be the return necessary to attract funds.

In addition to these factors, the company's capital structure itself affects the cost of capital. Interest payments on debt are an expense for tax purposes, so the payment of interest decreases the tax liability of the firm and therefore lowers the effective cost of debt. Further, debt is normally seen as a less risky investment than equity and normally carries an interest rate lower than the return expected by equity holders. Therefore, the inclusion of debt generally tends to lower the cost of capital. On the other hand, the greater the ratio of debt to equity, the greater the risk of default and the higher the return investors will require as compensation for the additional risk. This factor tends to increase the cost of capital. The goal of capital structure management is to create the combination of various sources of funds that trades off between debt and equity to create the lowest possible cost of capital.

In this chapter, you learn how to estimate the costs of various sources of funds and how taxes affect these costs. You then learn how to combine the costs of various sources of funds in order to develop an estimate of the average cost of capital for the firm.

A. COST OF CAPITAL CONCEPTS

1. For clarity in establishing cost of capital concepts, taxes will be ignored for the moment but will be introduced later. Suppose you have just decided to start a business. You have no money of your own but you can borrow an unlimited amount from your uncle at a 5% interest rate. In order to meet your obligation to your uncle, it will be necessary to invest in assets earning at least a _____ % return.

2. This required rate of return is frequently referred to as the *cost of capital* for your firm.

3. The cost of capital for the firm described above is _____ %.

4. For a slightly more realistic example, assume that the bank will loan $1 for each dollar of equity you have. You have no money of your own but can raise equity by selling stock to other people. A number of people have

---

1. 5%

3. 5%

expressed interest in your operation and will buy stock if they can expect at least 10% return on their investment. The bank will charge 5% interest on the loan. (Your company pays no taxes.)

You decide to go into business by selling $1,000 worth of stock and borrowing $1,000 from the bank. You will need to earn a minimum return of _____ % on the $2,000 if you wish to keep both the bank and the stockholders happy.

Skip to Frame 6 if you got the correct answer.

5. You will need to earn at least .05 × $1000 = *$50* a year on the $1000 borrowed from the bank and .10 × $1000 = *$100* on the $1000 raised by selling stock. You will, therefore, need to earn a total of $150 a year on a $2000 investment or:

150/2000 = .075 = 7½%

6. A more formal way to state the solution to Frame 4 is:

Item	Cost		Proportion		
Debt	.05	×	.5	=	.025
Equity	.05	×	.5	=	.050
					.075 or 7.5%

7. The required rate of return, as computed above, is frequently referred to as the *weighted average cost of capital* because it is computed by multiplying the cost of each source of funds by its "weight" or proportion of total sources of funds.

8. The required return on debt is normally referred to as the *cost of debt* and the required return on equity is referred to as the *cost of equity.*

9. Suppose the bank would loan you $2 for every dollar of equity. The bank would want a 6% return because its risks go up as your ratio of debt to equity goes up. Your stockholders would now require a 12% return because their investment is more risky. Your cost of capital in this case would be _____ .

---

4. 7.5%   **9.** 8%

Skip to Frame 11 if you got the correct answer.

10. The solution to Frame 9 is as follows:

Item	Cost	Proportion		Weighted Cost
Debt	.06	.667	=	.04
Equity	.12	.333	=	.04
Weighted Average Cost of Capital			=	.08 or 8%

A more intuitive approach is as follows: Suppose you decide to raise a total of $3000. If you raise $1000 in equity and $2000 in debt, you will need to earn .12 × $1000 = $120 on the equity portion and .06 × $2000 = $120 on the debt portion. The cost of capital would then be:

$$\frac{120 + 120}{3000} = \frac{240}{3000} = .08 \text{ or } 8\%$$

11. Suppose that the equity holders required a 12% return but the bank would still loan money at 5% with the 2/1 debt-to-equity ratio. What would the weighted average cost of capital be in this case?

B. TAX CONSIDERATIONS

12. Unfortunately, few businesses operate in a tax free world. Therefore, it will be necessary to consider the tax implications of debt and equity financing. As you may recall, interest payments are tax deductible expenses but profits, which are the stockholders' share of returns, are taxable.

13. A company has debt but no equity. The interest on the debt is 5%. The company would need to earn a return of _____ % on its investments *before* tax and interest to satisfy the lender.

Skip to Frame 15 if you got the correct answer.

---

11. .05 × .67 = .033
    .12 × .33 = .040
        .073 or 7.3% weighted average cost of capital

13. 5%

14. If the company earns only 5% on its investments, it will use all the earnings to pay interest and will have zero income before taxes. This will be sufficient to satisfy the lender.

15. Suppose a company is financed entirely by equity and the stockholders require a 10% return on their investment. If the company has a 50% average income tax rate, it would need to earn at least _____ % before taxes in order to have the required 10% after taxes.

Skip to Frame 17 if you got the correct answer.

16. Suppose you raise $1000 by selling stock. You will need to have $100 after-tax return to provide the required 10%. Therefore, you will need a $200 before-tax return to pay 50% in taxes and have $100 left.

Profit before tax	$200
Tax (.50 X $200)	100
Profit after tax	$100

$$\text{After-tax return} = \frac{100}{1000} = 10\% \quad \text{Before-tax return} = \frac{200}{1000} = 20\%$$

17. It is now possible to talk in terms of before-tax and after-tax cost of capital. For the company described in Frame 15, the required rate of return before tax is _____%, and the required after-tax rate of return is _____%.

18. In order to compare the cost of debt financing and the cost of equity financing, it is necessary to place all costs on a before-tax or after-tax basis. For several reasons, it is more helpful to place all costs on an after-tax basis.

19. Suppose you borrow $1000 at 6%. You must earn $ _____ before tax and interest if you are to cover the cost of the debt.

---

15. 20%

17. 20%
    10%

19. $60

Refer again to Frames 13 and 14 if you did not get the correct answer.

20. If the tax rate is 40%, $60 earnings before tax will leave $ _____ earnings after tax.

Skip to Frame 22 if you got the correct answer.

21. If the tax rate is 40%, $1.00 before tax will leave 60¢ after tax. Therefore, you only need to earn 60% as much per dollar of debt cost as you need per dollar of equity cost.

22. We can, therefore, say that the *after-tax cost of debt* is $^{36}/_{1000}$ = _____ % or .06 × (1 − .40) = _____ %.

23. The bank will loan your company $2 for every dollar of equity. The bank requires 6% interest and your stockholders require a 12% return on their investment. If the tax rate is 50%, the after-tax cost of debt is _____ %, and the after-tax cost of equity is _____ %.

24. Compute the weighted average cost of capital for the above problem.

Item	After-Tax Cost		Weight		Weighted Cost
Debt	_____	X	_____	=	_____
Equity	_____	X	_____	=	_____
	Weighted Average Cost			=	_____

Skip to Frame 27 if you got the correct answer.

25. You will notice that this is the same approach used in Frames 6 and 10 with the following two exceptions:

    a. The word "weight" is substituted for "proportion."

    b. After-tax costs are used since the effect of taxes must be considered.

---

20. $36

22. 3.6%
    3.6%

23. 3%
    12%

24. .03 × .67 = .02
    .12 × .33 = .04
    .06   .06

26. ABC Corporation can raise $3 in debt for every $1 in equity. The company must pay 8% interest on debt, and the equity investors require a 12% return on their investment. The tax rate is 50%. Compute the after-tax weighted average cost of capital.

Item	After-Tax Cost	Weight	Weighted Cost
Debt	_____	X ____ =	_____
Equity	_____	X ____ =	_____
	Weighted Average Cost	=	_____

27. You have decided to go into business and have two alternatives available with regard to capital structure. With ⅓ debt and ⅔ equity, investors will perceive the company as relatively safe. The required return for debt will be 6% and the required return for equity will be 9%. You could also finance the company with ½ debt and ½ equity. At this higher ratio of debt to equity, both the lenders and equity investors will perceive their investment as more risky. With this capital structure the required return on debt is estimated to be 8%, and the required return on equity is estimated to be 10%. The proposed company will be subject to a 25% income tax rate. Which capital structure will provide the lowest weighted average cost of capital?

28. If the proposed company in Frame 27 was subject to a 60% tax rate, which capital structure would provide the lowest weighted average cost of capital?

---

26. .04 X .75 = .03
   .12 X .25 = .03
   _____
   .06

27. .045 X 1/3 = .015   .06 X .5 = .03
   .090 X 2/3 = .060   .10 X .5 = .05
   _____   _____
   .075   .08

The weighted average cost of capital is lower with 1/3 debt.

28. .024 X 1/3 = .008   .032 X .5 = .016
   .090 X 2/3 = .060   .10 X .5 = .050
   _____   _____
   .068   .066

The weighted average cost of capital is lower with 1/2 debt.

29. Frames 27 and 28 illustrate that as the tax rate increases, the advantage of debt is greater. At higher tax rates, the company is likely to increase the proportion of debt to equity somewhat, even though it means that the company will be perceived as a more risky investment.

C. COST OF EQUITY

30. The cost of equity is the return required by holders of the common stock. The cost of equity is a function of the investment opportunities elsewhere and the perceived risk associated with that particular company's common stock. Unfortunately, it is seldom possible to directly observe the required return for equity investors. Some method of estimating their required return from available information must be used.

31. One widely used method for estimating the cost of existing equity is presented here. The formula is designed to use the market price of common stock to determine the return investors require. (The student is referred to any advanced finance text for a proof.)

$$K_e = D/P + g$$

where: K_e = Cost of equity (cost of common stock)
            D = Current dividend per share (annual)
            P = Current market price per share
            g = Expected constant annual growth rate of dividends
                  (expected to continue indefinitely)

32. A company's stock is currently selling for $40 a share. Dividends are $2 per share per year and are expected to grow at a rate of 4% a year. The cost of equity is:

$$K_e = \frac{2}{40} + .04 = \underline{\hspace{3cm}}$$

33. American Corporation's stock is currently selling for $50 a share. Dividends are $3 per share per year and are expected to grow at 4% a year. The cost of equity is _____ .

---

32. 9%

33. 10%

34. The required return on new equity is normally higher than the required return on existing equity. This difference in cost is caused by the fact that there are issue costs connected with the sale of additional stock. The return earned on new equity must be sufficiently high to offset the issue costs as well as earn a competitive rate of return.

35. The cost of new equity is represented by the formula:

$$K_{ne} = \frac{Ke}{1-c}$$

where: K_{ne} = cost of new equity

      c   = issue cost per share as a percent of market price per share

36. ABC Corporation's common stock has a market price of $50 per share. K_e for ABC is 10%. For a new issue of common stock, issue costs would be $5.00 per share. The cost of new equity is computed as follows:

c = 5/50 = .10

K_{ne} = .10/(1−.10) = _____

37. What would be the cost of new equity for ABC Corporation if issue costs were $10.00 per share instead of $5.00 per share?

38. Westek Corporation's common stock has a market value of $100 per share. Dividends are $5 per share and are expected to grow at a rate of 4% a year. Costs for a new issue would be $10 per share. Find the cost of existing equity and new equity for Westek.

D. COST OF PREFERRED STOCK

39. Preferred stock normally receives a set dividend and does not participate in earnings above this set dividend. The required return on preferred stock can therefore be estimated using the current market price.

K_P = D/P

where:

K_P	=	Cost of preferred stock
D	=	Dividends per share (annual)
P	=	Market price per share

---

36. 11.1%   **37.** c = .2   **38.** K_e = 9%

                        K_{ne} = 12.5%   c = .10

                                          K_{ne} = 10%

40. Westek Corporation has preferred stock outstanding that pays dividends of $8 a year and has a current market price of $100 a share. The cost of preferred stock is _____.

41. If the market price of Westek's preferred stock falls to $80 a share, the cost of preferred stock will rise to _____.

42. If you wish to issue new shares of preferred stock, the issue costs will make the cost of new preferred stock higher than the cost of existing preferred stock. The formula for the cost of new preferred stock is as follows:

$$K_{np} = \frac{K_p}{1-c}$$

where: c = issue cost per share of preferred stock as a percent of market price

43. Amtec Corporation has preferred stock outstanding with a cost of K_p = 9%. For a new issue, issue costs per share would be 10% of the market price per share. The cost of new preferred stock would be

_____.

44. Allied Corporation has preferred stock outstanding with a market price of $50 and an annual dividend of $4.50. Issue costs for a new issue would be $5.00 per share. Compute the cost of existing preferred stock and the cost of new preferred stock for Allied.

E. COST OF DEBT

45. The final type of financing to be treated is debt. Only bonds will be treated since the cost of other debt is normally determined by contacting lenders. As with common and preferred stock, the first step is to determine the return that existing investors are earning and then compute the cost of a new issue for the company.

---

40. 8%

41. 10%

43. 10%

44. K_e = 4.50/50 = .09
c = 5/50 = .10
K_{ne} = .09/(1−.1) = .10

46. Bonds pay a coupon or "face" interest rate which is stated as a percent of their principal value. The principal value is the price the issuing company will pay to redeem the bond at maturity. The number of years till maturity is, of course, part of the obligation of the company at the time the bond is first issued.

47. If a bond sells at its principal value, the before-tax cost, or yield, on the bond is simply the face interest rate. Frequently bonds sell at a price different than their principal value and the true return to buyers of the bonds will be different than the face rate. The before-tax cost of the bond issue is the yield that a buyer would earn at the current market price of the bond and is computed as follows:

$$K_d = \frac{iP + (P-M)/n}{(P+M)/2}$$

where: i = Face rate of interest
P = Principal value of the bond (normally $1,000)
M = Current market value of the bond
n = Number of years till maturity

48. American Corporation has bonds outstanding. The bonds have a face interest rate of 9% and a principal value of $1000. The bonds will mature in ten years, and have a current market value of $900 each. The before-tax cost of debt for American Corporation can be computed as follows:

$$K_d = \frac{90 + (1000-900)/10}{(1000+900)/2} = \frac{90+10}{950} = \underline{\qquad}\%$$

49. For the American Corporation bonds described above, assume that all information is the same except that the bonds will mature in twenty years. What is the before-tax cost of debt?

50. ABC Corporation has bonds outstanding. The bonds have a face interest rate of 7% and a principal value of $1000. They will mature in twenty years, and have a current market value of $800 each. Compute the before-tax cost of debt.

---

48. 10.53%

49. $\dfrac{90 + (1000-900)/20}{(1000+900)/2} = \dfrac{90+5}{950} = 10\%$

50. $\dfrac{70 + (1000-800)/20}{(1000+800)/2} = \dfrac{70+10}{900} = 8.89\%$

51. The same formula can be applied for a bond with a current market value above its principal value. For ABC Corporation (previous problem), assume that all information is the same except that the bonds have a current market value of $1200. What is the before-tax cost of debt?

Skip to Frame 53 if you got the correct answer.

52. Be sure that you understand how the answer to Frame 51 was computed before attempting this problem:
Americorp has bonds outstanding with a face interest rate of 11.5% and a principal value of $1000. The bonds will mature in ten years and they have a current market value of $1100. Compute the before-tax cost of debt.

53. As with preferred and common stock, the cost of a new debt issue is higher than the cost of existing funds. Due to the limited life of a bond, the formula for the cost of new debt is somewhat more complicated than the formula for the cost of new common and preferred stock. The formula for the cost of new debt is as follows:

$$K_{nd} = \frac{K_d + c/n}{1 - c/2}$$

where: c = Issue cost for a new bond issue as a percent of principal value

54. Great Eastern Corporation has a cost of existing debt equal to 10%. They are considering a new issue with a ten year period till maturity. The issue would be sold for a total price of $2,000,000 and issue costs would be $100,000 or _____% of principal value. The before-tax cost of new debt would be:

$$K_{nd} = \frac{.10 + .05/10}{1 - .05/2} = \frac{.10 + .005}{1 - .025} = \frac{.105}{.975} = \underline{\qquad}\%$$

---

51. $\dfrac{70 + (1000-1200)/20}{(1000+1200)/2} = \dfrac{70 - 10}{1100} = 5.45\%$

52. $K_d = \dfrac{115 + (1000-1100)/10}{(1000+1100)/2} = .10$

54. c = .05

$K_{nd} = 10.8\%$

55. Midwest Corporation has a cost of existing debt equal to 9% and is considering a new issue that will mature in 20 years. Issue costs would be 10% of principal value. The before-tax cost of new debt would be _____%.

56. Midway Corporation has an outstanding bond issue with 20 years remaining till maturity. The face interest rate is 9% and the current market price per bond is $900. The principal value per bond is $1000. A new issue with the same maturity date would have 5% issue costs. Compute the before-tax cost of existing debt and new debt for Midway Corporation.

57. As you will recall, the after-tax costs of various sources of funds were of primary interest. The formulas for the cost of common and preferred stock were on an after-tax basis. However, the formulas for the cost of debt were on a before-tax basis. To make the costs comparable, it is necessary to convert the cost of debt to an after-tax cost.

58. As you will recall, the after-tax cost of debt is lower because interest expense is tax deductible. The formulas for the after-tax cost of existing debt and new debt are as follows:

$K_d(\text{after-tax}) = K_d \times (1-T)$

$K_{nd}(\text{after-tax}) = K_{nd} \times (1-T)$

where: T = The tax rate faced by the company issuing the bonds

59. Assume that the tax rate for Midway Corporation (Frame 56) is 50%. The after-tax cost of existing and new debt would be:

$K_d(\text{after-tax}) = K_d \times (1-T) = .10 \times (1-.5) = $ _____

$K_{nd}(\text{after-tax}) = K_{nd} \times (1-T) = .105 \times (1-.5) = $ _____

---

55. $\dfrac{.09 + .1/20}{1 - .1/2} = 10\%$

56. $K_d = \dfrac{90 + (1000-900)/20}{(1000+900)/2} = 10\%$

$K_d = \dfrac{.10 + .05/20}{1 - .05/2} = 10.5\%$

59. K_d (after-tax) = .05

K_{nd} (after-tax) = .0525

60. ABC Corporation has an existing debt issue outstanding with an 8% face interest rate and 20 years till maturity. The bonds have a $1000 principal value and an $800 market price. Issue costs for a new issue would be 10%. ABC faces a 50% tax rate. Compute the before-tax and after-tax cost of existing and new debt.

Skip to Frame 62 if you got the correct answer.

61. Be sure you understand the answer to Frame 60 before attempting this problem:

Great American Corporation has an existing debt issue outstanding with 20 years till maturity and a face interest rate of 7.1%. The bonds have a $1000 principal value and an $800 market price. Issue costs for a new issue would be 10%. Great American faces a 50% tax rate. Compute the before-tax and after-tax cost of existing debt and new debt.

F. WEIGHTED AVERAGE COST OF CAPITAL

62. You are now ready to combine the after-tax costs of the individual sources of funds to come up with a weighted average cost of capital. You may wish to refresh your memory by briefly reviewing Section A of this chapter before proceeding.

---

60. $K_d \text{ (before-tax)} = \dfrac{80 + (1000-800)/20}{(1000+800)/2} = .10$

$K_{nd} \text{ (before-tax)} = \dfrac{.10 + .10/.20}{1 - .10/2} = .1105$

$K_d \text{ (after-tax)} = .10 \times (1-.5) = .05$
$K_d \text{ (after-tax)} = .1105 \times (1-.5) = .05525$

61. $K_d \text{ (before-tax)} = \dfrac{71 + (1000-800)/20}{(1000+800)/2} = .09$

$K_{nd} \text{ (before-tax)} = \dfrac{.09 + .10/20}{1 - .10/2} = .10$

$K_d \text{ (after-tax)} = .09 \times (1-.5) = .045$
$K_{nd} \text{ (after-tax)} = .10 \times (1-.5) = .05$

63. You will now compute the weighted average cost of capital in a manner similar to that used in Section A of this chapter. There are, however, two additional points to be observed at this stage. First, preferred stock has been added so that there are three rather than two sources of funds. Second, it is necessary to discern between existing and new funds.

64. You observed earlier that for each of the three sources of funds, the cost of new funds was *higher/lower* than the cost of existing funds. A company can, therefore, have two costs of capital, one for existing funds and one for new funds. We will start by looking at the cost of existing funds for a company.

65. Carousel Corporation has outstanding common stock with a market value of $100,000, preferred stock with a market value of $50,000, and debt with a market value of $50,000. _____ % of their funds are from common stock, _____ % are from preferred stock, and _____ % are from debt. The after-tax costs are as follows. Compute the weighted average cost of capital.

Item	Cost	Proportion	Weighted Cost
Debt	.04 X	=	
Preferred Stock	.08 X	=	
Common Stock	.10 X	=	_____
Weighted Average Cost		=	

---

64. higher

65. 50%, 25%, 25%

Item	Cost	Proportion	Weighted Cost
Debt	.04 X	.25	=	.01
Preferred Stock	.08 X	.25	=	.02
Common Stock	.10 X	.50	=	.05
Weighted Average Cost			=	.08

66. Americorp has outstanding common stock with a market value of $75,000, preferred stock with a market value of $25,000, and debt with a market value of $50,000. The after-tax cost of common stock is 12%, the after-tax cost of debt is 4.5%, and the after-tax cost of preferred stock is 9%. Compute the weighted average cost of capital for Americorp.

Skip to Frame 68 if you got the correct answer.

67. Midtek has outstanding common stock with a market value of $50,000, preferred stock with a market value of $50,000, and debt with a market value of $100,000. The after-tax costs of common stock, preferred stock, and debt are 12%, 8%, and 4% respectively. Compute the weighted average cost of capital for Midtek.

66.	*Item*	*Cost*		*Proportion*		*Weighted Cost*
	Debt	.045	X	.3333	=	.015
	Preferred Stock	.090	X	.1667	=	.015
	Common Stock	.120	X	.5000	=	.060
		Weighted Average Cost			=	.090

67.	*Item*	*Cost*		*Proportion*		*Weighted Cost*
	Debt	.04	X	.50	=	.02
	Preferred Stock	.08	X	.25	=	.02
	Common Stock	.12	X	.25	=	.03
		Average Weighted Cost			=	.07

68. ABC Corp. has outstanding common stock with a total market value of $100,000. Price per share is $100 and dividend per share is $6. Dividends are expected to grow at an annual rate of 6%. The company has preferred stock with a total market value of $50,000 and a market price per share of $80. Dividends per share of preferred stock are $8. The company has bonds outstanding with a market value of $50,000 and a market price of $800 per bond. The bonds have 20 years till maturity and a face interest rate of 6.2% on the $1,000 principal value per bond. ABC faces a 50% tax rate. Compute the weighted average cost of capital for ABC.

Skip to Frame 70 if you got the correct answer.

68.	Item	Cost	Proportion	Weighted Cost
	Debt	.04 X	.25 =	.010
	Preferred Stock	.10 X	.25 =	.025
	Common Stock	.12 X	.50 =	.060
		Weighted Average Cost	=	.095

69. Be sure you understand the answer to Frame 68 before attempting this problem:

Florida Corporation has common stock outstanding with a total market value of $100,000 and a price per share of $100. Dividends are $6 a year and are expected to grow at an annual rate of 8%. The company has preferred stock outstanding with a total market price of $50,000 and a market price per share of $80. Dividends per share of preferred stock are $8. The company also has bonds outstanding with a market value totalling $50,000. Principal value per bond is $1000 and market value per bond is $800. The bonds have 20 years till maturity and pay a face interest rate of 7.1%. Florida Corp. faces a 50% tax rate. Compute the weighted average cost of capital.

70. The cost of new funds is applicable when the company has committed all existing funds and is considering going outside for additional funds. For simplicity, we will assume throughout this section that the mix of common stock, preferred stock, and debt will be the same for new funds as for the existing capital structure.

69.

Item	Cost	Proportion		Weighted Cost
Debt	.045 X	.25	=	.0113
Preferred Stock	.100 X	.25	=	.0250
Common Stock	.140 X	.50	=	.0700
	Weighted Average Cost		=	.1063

71. Amalgamated Corporation has an existing capital structure as follows:

Debt: Before-tax cost: 9%
Years till maturity: 20
Market value of existing bonds: $100,000
Issue cost for a new issue of bonds: 10%

Preferred Stock: After-tax cost: 9%
Market value of existing preferred: $100,000
Issue cost for a new issue of preferred: 10%

Common Stock: After-tax cost: 12%
Market value of existing common stock: $300,000
Issue cost for a new issue of common: 20%

Amalgamated Corp. is subject to a 50% marginal tax rate. The before-tax cost of new debt would be (a) _____ . The after-tax cost of new debt would be (b) _____ . The after-tax cost of new preferred stock is (c) _____ . The after-tax cost of new common stock is (d) _____ .

If you missed part a or b, review Frames 53 to 61. If you missed part c, review Frames 42 to 44. If you missed part d, review Frames 35 to 37.

72. The weighted average after-tax cost of existing capital for Amalgamated Corporation (previous problem) is _____ , and the weighted average after-tax cost of new capital would be _____ if the company decides to expand beyond the limits of existing capital.

Skip to Frame 76 if you got the correct answers to Frames 71 and 72.

---

71. (a) $(.09 + .1/20) / (1-.1/2) = .10$
(b) $.10(1 - .5) = .05$
(c) $.09/(1 - .1) = .10$
(d) $.12/(1 - .20) = .15$

72. Weighted average after-tax cost of existing capital: *9.9%*
Weighted average cost of new capital: *12%*

73. The weighted average after-tax cost of existing capital for Amalgamated Corporation is computed as follows:

Item	After-tax Cost	Weight	Weighted Cost
Debt	.045	.2	.009
Preferred Stock	.090	.2	.018
Common Stock	.120	.6	.072

Weighted Average Cost = $\underline{.099}$

The weighted average after-tax cost of new capital is computed as follows:

Item	After-tax Cost	Weight	Weighted Cost
Debt	.05	.2	.01
Preferred Stock	.10	.2	.02
Common Stock	.15	.6	.09
			.12

74. Midway Corporation has an existing capital structure as shown below. Midway is subject to a 50% marginal tax rate.

Debt: Before-tax cost: 8.8%
                     Years till maturity: 10
                     Market value of existing bonds: $2,000,000
                     Issue cost for a new issue of bonds: 8%

Preferred Stock: After-tax cost: 10.8%
                     Market value of existing preferred: $1,000,000
                     Issue cost for a new issue of preferred: 10%

Common Stock: After-tax cost: 13.2%
                     Market value of existing common stock: $2,000,000
                     Issue cost for a new issue of common: 12%

The before-tax cost of new debt would be _____ .
The after-tax cost of new debt would be _____ .
The after-tax cost of new preferred stock would be _____ .
The after-tax cost of new common stock would be _____ .

---

74. $(.088 + .08/10)/(1 - .08/2) = .10$ $.108/(1 - .10) = .12$
      $10(1 - .5) = 05$ $.132/(1 - .12) = .15$

75. The weighted average after-tax cost of existing capital for Midway Corporation is _____, and the weighted average after-tax cost of new capital would be _____.

76. Refer back to Frame 72. For Amalgamated Corporation, the weighted average after-tax cost of existing capital is _____ and the weighted average after-tax cost of new capital would be _____. Amalgamated Corporation has $10,000 in cash currently available for investment. The after-tax cost of these funds would equal the cost of existing capital or _____. If they wish to invest additional funds beyond the $10,000, they will need to go to outside sources and the cost of these new funds will be _____.

77. The weighted average cost of capital is not the same at all levels but will *rise/fall* if Amalgamated seeks outside funds to finance additional investments.

G. ALTERNATE APPROACHES TO THE COST OF EQUITY CAPITAL

78. The material in this section is optional. You may skip directly to the review with no loss in continuity.

79. As mentioned earlier, the estimation of the cost of existing equity is the most difficult portion of the cost of capital calculation in practice. This section will explain two alternate methods of estimating the cost of equity capital.

---

75. Cost of existing capital
$.044 \times .4 = .0176$
$.108 \times .2 = .0216$
$.132 \times .4 = \underline{.0528}$
$.0920$

Cost of new capital
$.05 \times .4 = .020$
$.12 \times .2 = .024$
$.15 \times .4 = \underline{.060}$
$.104$

76. 9.9%
12%
9.9%
12%

77. rise

80. Earnings per share of common stock are particularly important in corporate finance. It is argued that the earnings per share are the real return to the shareholder whether they are paid out in the form of dividends or reinvested for his benefit. Furthermore, investors watch the changes in earnings closely and the company frequently feels that it must take no action which will lead to a decline in earnings per share. Therefore it is frequently argued that earnings per share divided by market price is the shareholders' return or the required return on equity.

81. ABC Corporation has earnings per share of $5 and the market price of a share of ABC stock is currently $50. Using the earnings per share approach, the required return on equity is _____.

82. XYZ Corporation had no profits last year but actually suffered a loss of $3 per share. XYZ's stock is currently being traded for $9 per share. Using the earnings approach, the required return on equity for XYZ is _____.

83. Frame 82 points up one serious limitation of the earnings per share approach. Investors in stock do not make decisions based solely on last year's earnings per share. They act based on expected future earnings per share. This leads to problems in interpretation. The earnings per share approach has further limitations but a discussion of these is beyond the scope of this treatment.

84. Another approach to the cost of equity capital emanates from the required rate of return discussion in section E of Chapter 7. If you have not completed that section, do so before continuing. That section can be completed independently of the rest of Chapter 7.

85. The relationship between risk and required rate of return was developed in the above mentioned section. That relationship is stated in equation form in Frame 63 of Chapter 7 as follows:

$Ke = R + b(Em - R)$

where: Ke = required rate of return   b = beta
         R = risk-free interest rate   Em = expected average return for the stock market in general

From your study of the cost of capital, you now realize that this estimated required rate of return (Ke) is the estimated cost of equity.

81. 5/50 = 10%   82. indeterminate

86. Midatlantic Power is a relatively stable company with a beta of 0.5. Earnings per share for the company were $2.50 last year and dividends per share were $2.00. No growth in dividends is anticipated. The risk-free interest rate is 6% and average expected return for the stock market in general is estimated to be 9%. The common stock of Midatlantic is currently selling at $25 per share. Estimate the cost of equity for Midatlantic using each of the methods discussed: dividend growth, earnings per share, and risk-adjusted rate of return.

87. New Corporation has a beta of 1.5. The stock is selling for $20 per share and earnings per share are $2.00. Dividends per share are $1.00 and are expected to grow at 6% per year. Based on a 6% risk-free interest rate and estimated average returns for the stock market of 9%, estimate the cost of equity for New Corporation using each of the three methods.

88. The various approaches to estimating the cost of equity usually *do/do not* give identical results. The analyst therefore faces a difficult problem in deciding which estimate to use. Opinions on the solution to this problem vary widely among finance scholars and practitioners.

89. The practitioner cannot wait until the theoretical problems are solved to make a decision. Some method of estimating the cost of equity must be used in the meantime. If dividend growth is quite stable for the company under study, the dividend growth approach can be used with some degree of confidence. Under some stable conditions the earnings per share approach can be used. If these methods cannot be used, one frequent approach is to use a simplification of the risk-adjusted rate of return method. Long run stock market returns are first estimated and then the required rate of return is moved up or down from the average return for

---

86. Dividend growth: $Ke = 2/25 + 0 = 8\%$
    Earnings per share: $Ke = \$2.50/\$25 = 10\%$
    Risk-adjusted rate of return: $Ke = .06 + .5(.09 - .06) = 7.5\%$

87. Dividend growth: $Ke = 1/20 + .06 = 11\%$
    Earnings per share: $Ke = 2/20 = 10\%$
    Risk-adjusted rate of return: $Ke = .06 + 1.5(.09 - .06) = 10.5\%$

88. do not

the market depending on whether the particular company is more or less risky than average. The amount of such adjustment frequently relies as much on intuition as on analysis.

90. Whatever method is used for estimating the cost of equity, it must be remembered that the result is only an *estimate*. As with all estimates, some margin for error must be allowed.

SUMMARY

A. COST OF CAPITAL CONCEPT

The cost of capital is the rate of return a firm must earn on its investments in order to satisfy the investors who furnished or will furnish capital to the firm. Each source of capital (i.e., debt, preferred stock, common stock) has a cost in terms of a rate of return required by the group of investors holding these particular instruments. The company should select only those investments which are expected to earn a return at least equal to an average of the returns required by the various investor groups.

B. TAX CONSIDERATIONS

It is necessary to state all capital costs on an after-tax basis. Since interest is a tax deductible expense, the after-tax cost of debt is computed as follows:

$$K_d(\text{after-tax}) = (1 - T) \times K_d(\text{before-tax})$$

where: K_d = Cost of debt
T = Marginal tax rate of the firm

C. COST OF EQUITY

$$K_e = D/P + g$$

where: K_e = Cost of existing equity (or common stock)
D = Dividends per share per year
P = Market price per share
g = Expected continuous annual growth rate in dividends per share

$$K_{ne} = K_e /(1{-}c)$$

where: K_{ne} = Cost of new equity
c = Issue cost per share as a percent of market price per share

D. COST OF PREFERRED STOCK

$K_p = D/P$

where: D = Dividends per share per year

P = Market price per share

$K_{np} = K_p/(1-c)$

where: K_{np} = Cost of new preferred stock

c = Issue cost per share of preferred stock as a percent of market price

E. COST OF DEBT

$$K_d = \frac{iP + (P-M)/n}{(P+M)/2}$$

where: K_d = Cost of debt

i = Face rate of interest

P = Principal value of the bond (normally $1,000)

M = Current market value of the bond

n = Number of years till maturity

$$K_{nd} = \frac{K_d + c/n}{1 - c/2}$$

where: K_{nd} = Cost of new debt

c = Issue cost for a new bond issue as a percent of principal value

F. WEIGHTED AVERAGE COST OF CAPITAL

After the costs of the various sources of funds are determined, these costs must be combined into an average cost of capital. Since each component is "weighted" according to the proportion of total capital it represents, this is referred to as the weighted average cost of capital. The "weighted cost" of each component is computed by multiplying the after-tax cost of that component by the percent of total market value of capital sources represented by that particular component. The weighted costs of the individual components are then added to compute the weighted average cost of capital.

G. COST OF EXISTING CAPITAL AND COST OF NEW CAPITAL

Since there are issue costs involved in raising outside capital, the cost of new capital is greater than the cost of existing capital. The company therefore faces a "cost of capital curve" with the weighted average cost of capital going up when it is forced to go outside for additional funds in order to accept additional investments.

H. ALTERNATE APPROACHES TO THE COST OF EQUITY CAPITAL (OPTIONAL)

In addition to the formula presented in (C), the following two formulas are also sometimes used to estimate the cost of equity:

$Ke = EPS/P$

where: EPS = Earnings per share
           P   = Market price per share

$Ke = R + b(Em - R)$

where: R   = risk-free interest rate
         b   = beta
        Em = expected average return for the stock market in general

PROBLEMS

PROBLEM 1:

ABC Corporation has the capital structure shown below. The company is subject to a 50% tax rate on regular income. Compute the before-tax and after-tax cost of debt, the after-tax cost of preferred stock, and the after-tax cost of common stock.

Debt: Market Value: $2,000,000
                    Face interest rate: 7.1%
                    Market price per bond: $800
                    Principal value per bond: $1,000
                    Years till maturity: 20

Preferred Stock: Market value: $1,000,000
                    Market price per share: $100
                    Annual dividend per share: $9

Common Stock: Market value: $1,000,000
                    Market price per share: $80
                    Annual dividend per share: $4
                    Expected continuous annual growth rate in
                    dividends: 7%

PROBLEM 2:

Compute the after-tax weighted average cost of capital for ABC Corporation.

PROBLEM 3:

For ABC Corporation, issue costs for new issues would be as follows:

Debt: 10% of principal value

Preferred Stock: 10% of market price per share
Common Stock: 20% of market price per share

Compute the before-tax and after-tax cost of new debt, the after-tax cost of new preferred stock, and the after-tax cost of new common stock for ABC.

PROBLEM 4:

Compute the weighted average after-tax cost of new capital for ABC Corp.

SOLUTIONS

SOLUTION 1:

Cost of debt (before tax)

$$K_d = \frac{.071 \times 1000 + (1000-800)/20}{(1000+800)/2} = \frac{71+10}{900} = \underline{\underline{9\%}}$$

Cost of debt (after tax)

$K_d(\text{after-tax}) = .09(1-.50) = .045 = \underline{\underline{4.5\%}}$

Cost of preferred stock

$K_p = 9/100 = \underline{\underline{9\%}}$

Cost of common stock (cost of equity)

$K_e = 4/80 + .07 = 12\%$

SOLUTION 2:

Item	After-tax Cost	Weight	Weighted Cost
Debt	.045	.50	.0225
Preferred Stock	.090	.25	.0225
Common Stock	.120	.25	.0300
	Weighted Average Cost =		.075

SOLUTION 3:

Cost of new debt (before tax)

$$K_{nd} = \frac{.09 + .1/20}{1 - .1/20} = \underline{10\%}$$

Cost of new debt (after tax)

$$K_{nd}(\text{after tax}) = .10(1-.50) = \underline{5\%}$$

Cost of new preferred stock

$$K_{np} = \frac{.09}{1 - .1} = 10\%$$

Cost of new common stock (cost of new equity)

$$K_{ne} = \frac{.12}{1 - .2} = \underline{15\%}$$

SOLUTION 4:

Cost of new capital

Item	After-tax Cost	Weight	Weighted Cost
Debt	.05	.50	.0250
Preferred Stock	.10	.25	.0250
Common Stock	.15	.25	.0375
			.0875

CONCLUSION

The various areas of financial analysis and decision making are not independent but closely related. The financial manager must deal with various interrelated effects of each financial decision. The purpose of this concluding comment is to highlight this interrelated nature of financial decision making.

Since wealth maximization is the stated goal of financial management, value is central to all financial decision making. The value of the shareholders' wealth is affected by the profitability with which assets are invested, the timing of returns, and the risk associated with these returns. In addition, the capital structure of the firm affects the degree to which these returns result in profitability for the owners and enhance the value of the owners' investment.

Throughout this volume, the emphasis has been on the effect of financial decisions on profitability, risk, and subsequent value. Financial statement analysis, in addition to other uses, is a valuable tool for analyzing the profitability and risk results of past operations. Pro-forma analysis is valuable for projecting future returns and risk, as well as testing the risk-return effects of various strategies. Leverage was studied because it has important effects on the profitability and risk of the firm. In the leverage chapter (page 51), the relationship between the operating characteristics of the firm and its capital structure were pointed out for the first time. Working capital management also affects the risk-return structure of the firm, and under this topic the effect of the current asset structure on the liability structure of the firm was analyzed. Time value of money provided the necessary tools to understand the effect of the timing of returns on value and provided the basis for capital budgeting techniques directed toward the goal of maximizing value. In the chapter on value (page 165), the relationship between the riskiness of the assets and the required rate of return, or cost of funds was discussed as well as the basic principles of asset valuation. Finally, the estimation of the cost of funds to the firm was developed; it was earlier shown that the cost of funds to the firm was an important consideration in maximizing the value of the firm.

It is not possible to make a financial decision in one area while ignoring the effects of that decision in other areas. The manager must continually be aware of the complex interrelationships and the various effects of each decision. Due to the complex nature of the decisions under investigation, it is seldom possible to reduce financial decisions to simple mathematical problems with a solution to which every competent analyst would concur. While it is hoped that this volume will provide a good basic understanding of the techniques of financial analysis and deicison making, it will not act as a substitute for the seasoned judgement that will come only from applying these techniques to the analysis of actual business decisions.

TABLE I / Future Value of a Single Amount $(1+r)^n$

Years	2%	4%	5%	6%	8%	10%	12%	14%	16%
1	1.020	1.040	1.050	1.060	1.080	1.100	1.120	1.140	1.160
2	1.040	1.082	1.102	1.124	1.166	1.210	1.254	1.300	1.346
3	1.061	1.124	1.158	1.191	1.260	1.331	1.405	1.482	1.561
4	1.082	1.170	1.216	1.262	1.360	1.464	1.574	1.689	1.811
5	1.104	1.217	1.276	1.338	1.469	1.611	1.762	1.925	2.100
6	1.126	1.265	1.340	1.419	1.587	1.772	1.974	2.195	2.436
7	1.149	1.316	1.407	1.504	1.714	1.949	2.211	2.502	2.826
8	1.172	1.369	1.477	1.594	1.851	2.144	2.476	2.853	3.278
9	1.195	1.423	1.551	1.689	1.999	2.358	2.773	3.252	3.803
10	1.219	1.480	1.629	1.791	2.159	2.594	3.106	3.707	4.411
11	1.243	1.539	1.710	1.898	2.332	2.853	3.479	4.226	5.117
12	1.268	1.601	1.796	2.012	2.518	3.138	3,896	4,818	5.936
13	1.294	1.665	1.886	2.133	2.720	3.452	4.363	5.492	6.886
14	1.319	1.732	1.980	2.261	2.937	3.797	4.887	6.261	7.988
15	1.346	1.801	2.079	2.397	3.172	4.177	5.474	7.138	9.266
20	1.486	2.191	2.653	3.207	4.661	6,727	9.646	13.743	19.461
25	1.641	2.666	3.386	4.292	6.848	10.835	17.000	26.462	40.874
30	1.811	3.243	4.322	5.743	10.063	17.449	29.960	50.950	85.850

TABLE II / Present Value of a Single Amount $\dfrac{1}{(1+r)^n}$

years	2%	4%	5%	6%	8%	10%	12%	14%	16%
1	.980	.962	.952	.943	.926	.909	.893	.877	.862
2	.961	.925	.907	.890	.857	.826	.797	.769	.743
3	.942	.889	.864	.840	.794	.751	.712	.675	.641
4	.924	.855	.823	.792	.735	.683	.636	.592	.552
5	.906	.822	.784	.747	.681	.621	.567	.519	.476
6	.888	.790	.746	.705	.630	.564	.507	.456	.410
7	.871	.760	.711	.665	.583	.513	.452	.400	.354
8	.853	.731	.677	.627	.540	.467	.404	.351	.305
9	.837	.703	.645	.592	.500	.424	.361	.308	.263
10	.820	.676	.614	.558	.463	.386	.322	.270	.227
11	.804	.650	.585	.527	.429	.350	.287	.237	.195
12	.788	.625	.557	.497	.397	.319	.257	.208	.168
13	.773	.601	.530	.469	.368	.290	.229	.182	.145
14	.758	.577	.505	.442	.340	.263	.205	.160	.125
15	.743	.555	.481	.417	.315	.239	.183	.140	.108
20	.673	.456	.377	.312	.215	.149	.104	.073	.051
25	.610	.375	.295	.233	.146	.092	.059	.038	.024
30	.552	.308	.231	.174	.099	.057	.033	.020	.012

TABLE III / Future Value of a Stream of Payments

Years	2%	4%	5%	6%	8%	10%	12%	14%	16%
1	1.000	1.000	1.000	1.000	1.000	1.000	1.000	1.000	1.000
2	2.020	2.040	2.050	2.060	2.080	2.100	2.120	2.140	2.160
3	3.060	3.122	3.152	3.184	3.246	3.310	3.374	3.440	3.506
4	4.122	4.246	4.310	4.375	4.506	4.641	4.779	4.921	5.066
5	5.204	5.416	5.526	5.637	5.867	6.105	6.353	6.610	6.877
6	6.308	6.633	6.802	6.975	7.336	7.716	8.115	8.536	8.977
7	7.434	7.898	8.142	8.394	8.923	9.487	10.089	10.730	11.414
8	8.583	9.214	9.549	9.897	10.637	11.436	12.300	13.233	14.240
9	9.755	10.583	11.027	11.491	12.488	13.579	14.776	16.085	17.519
10	10.950	12.006	12.578	13.181	14.487	15.937	17.549	19.337	21.321
11	12.169	13.486	14.207	14.972	16.645	18.531	20.655	23.045	25.733
12	13.412	15.026	15.917	16.870	18.977	21.384	24.133	27.271	30.850
13	14.680	16.627	17.713	18.882	21.495	24.523	28.029	32.089	36.786
14	15.974	18.292	19.599	21.015	24.215	27.975	32.393	37.581	43.672
15	17.293	20.024	21.579	23.276	27.152	31.772	37.280	43.842	51.660
20	24.297	29.778	33.066	36.786	45.762	57.275	72.052	91.025	115.380
25	32.030	41.646	47.727	54.864	73.106	98.347	133.334	181.871	249.214
30	40.568	56.085	66.439	79.058	113.283	164.494	241.333	356.787	530.312

TABLE IV / Present Value of a Stream of Payments

Years	2%	4%	5%	6%	8%	10%	12%	14%	16%
1	.980	.962	.952	.943	.926	.909	.893	.877	.862
2	1.942	1.886	1.859	1.833	1.783	1.736	1.690	1.647	1.605
3	2.884	2.775	2.723	2.673	2.577	2.487	2.402	2.322	2.246
4	3.808	3.630	3.546	3.465	3.312	3.170	3.037	2.914	2.798
5	4.713	4.452	4.329	4.212	3.993	3.791	3.605	3.433	3.274
6	5.601	5.242	5.076	4.917	4.623	4.355	4.111	3.889	3.685
7	6.472	6.002	5.786	5.582	5.206	4.868	4.564	4.288	4.039
8	7.325	6.733	6.463	6.210	5.747	5.335	4.968	4.639	4.344
9	8.162	7.435	7.108	6.802	6.247	5.759	5.328	4.946	4.607
10	8.983	8.111	7.722	7.360	6.710	6.145	5.650	5.216	4.833
11	9.787	8.760	8.306	7.887	7.139	6.495	5.938	5.453	5.029
12	10.575	9.385	8.863	8.384	7.536	6.814	6.194	5.660	5.197
13	11.384	9.986	9.394	8.853	7.904	7.103	6.424	5.842	5.342
14	12.106	10.563	9.899	9.295	8.244	7.367	6.628	6.002	5.468
15	12.849	11.118	10.380	9.712	8.559	7.606	6.811	6.142	5.575
20	16.351	13.590	12.462	11.470	9.818	8.514	7.469	6.623	5.929
25	19.523	15.622	14.094	12.783	10.675	9.077	7.843	6.873	6.097
30	22.396	17.292	15.372	13.765	11.258	9.427	8.055	7.003	6.177